A você a men
Dom Inácio
res espiritua

João Teixeira de Faria
PRESIDENTE DA CASA DE DOM INÁCIO

SPIRITUAL CURES

ABDR
ASSOCIAÇÃO BRASILEIRA DE DIREITOS REPROGRÁFICOS
CÓPIA NÃO AUTORIZADA É CRIME · RESPEITE O DIREITO AUTORAL

EDITORA AFILIADA

ISMAR ESTULANO GARCIA

SPIRITUAL CURES

Edition
2007

AB
EDITORA
Cultura e Qualidade

Cover: Elton Oliveira Amaral
José Sérgio de Sousa
Maurício Luzia de Oliveira

Composition: Elton Oliveira Amaral
José Sérgio de Souza
Maurício Luzia de Oliveira

Proofreaders: Dheyne de Souza Santos
Ismar Estulano Garcia
Gisele Dionísio da Silva

Editor-in-chief: Maurício Luzia de Oliveira

CIP-Brazil Cataloging - in - Publication Data

	Garcia, Ismar Estulano
G216s	Spiritual Cures / Ismar Estulano Garcia. Tr. Gisele Dionísio da Silva – Goiânia: AB, 2007.

224 p.

ISBN 978-85-7498-155-0

1. Spiritual Healing 2. Dom Inacio's – Activities 3. João de Deus - Biography 4. Brazilian Law – Spiritual Healing 5. Medium - Caricteristic 6. Psychography – Judicial prool I. Title.

CDU: 139.9:615.855
139.9:929
331.47

AB Editora
Cultura e Qualidade
Vendas: (62) 3219-8600
Informações: (62) 3219-8696
Fax: (62) 3219-8644

www.abeditora.com.br
abeditora@abeditora.com.br • livros@abeditora.com.br

Rua 15, n. 252 • Centro • CEP: 74030-030 • Goiânia-GO

Translation:
Gisele Dionísio da Silva

The English version of *Curas Espirituais (Spiritual Cures)* received valuable support from **Diego Copola** and **Euler Nunes Barbosa** – volunteers at Casa de Dom Inácio.

CONTENTS

CHAPTER I
INTRODUCTION 1
1. The book 3
2. Absence of religious confrontation 12
3. Absence of scientific confrontation 13
4. Absence of juridical confrontation 16
5. Medium and mediumship 17
6. Commenting on spiritual cures 20
7. Other information 22

CHAPTER II
JOÃO DE DEUS 27
1. Family 29
2. Ordinary citizen 30
3. Wanderings 33
4. Mediumship 35
5. Prescribed medication 39
6. Other information 40

CHAPTER III
CASA DE DOM INÁCIO 45
1. Abadiânia 47
2. Casa de Dom Inácio – what is it like? 49
3. Physical space 51
4. Parking lot 52
5. Rest area 52
6. Mediumistic area 53
7. Administrative area and staff 56
8. Snack bar 58
9. Bookshop 58
10. Regular visitors 59

11. Foreigners 63
12. Travel groups and guides.. 64
13. Infiltration 65
14. Service procedures 67
15. Assistant mediums, sons and daughters of the Casa 68
16. Opening of procedures and service queues 69
17. Entity services 71
18. Casa colors and white clothes 73
19. Indoor environment 74
20. Medication 75
21. Photography and filming... 75
22.Closing of procedures 77
23. Soup distribution 77
24. Casa da Alimentação (Feeding Home) 78
25. Waterfall baths and crystal baths 80
26. Communication 80
27. Income and expenses... 81
28. Other information.. 82

CHAPTER IV
ENTITIES 87
1. Initial comments.. 89
2. Incorporation and de-incorporation................................. 89
3. Entities 90
4. Communication 91
5. Infiltration and Identification 91
6. Famous Entities 92

CHAPTER V
SPIRITUAL CURES 105
1. Initial measures 107
2. Frauds in spiritual healing 107
3. Procedures in spiritual healing 109
4. Attendance in spiritual healing....................................... 110
5. Eliminated disease and paralyzed disease 118
6. Individual and group surgeries 118
7. Spiritual healing involving cuts 120

8. Number of surgery patients 121
9. Duration of surgeries 122
10. Review and discharge 122
11. Rest and post-surgery 123
12. Recurrence 124
13. Medication 125
14. Curious references 126
15. Illness and impossibility of pregnancy 127
16. Desperate and terminal patients 128
17. Attendance outside Abadiânia 129
18. Real stories of spiritual cures 131

CHAPTER VI
SPIRITUAL MANIFESTATIONS AND BRAZILIAN LAW 175
1. Religious freedom 177
2. Law 177
3. Penal Code 178
4. Typification 179
5. Malice and negligence 182
6. Attempt 183
7. Aiding and Abetting 183
8. Public penal action 184
9. Criminal instruction and judgment 184
10. Anticipated judgment 186
11. Prescription 187
12. Crimes of lesser offensive potential 188
13. Appeal 189
14. Psychography and copyright 190
15. Psychography as judicial proof 193
16. Zé Arigó 196
17. Criminally-sued famous mediums 197
18. Doctrinal opinions 198
19. Judicial decisions 200

THE AUTHOR 203

REFERENCES 207

Chapter I

Introduction

In this introduction general references are made regarding the author, this book, mediums and mediumship, Casa de Dom Inácio and cures performed there, as well as other useful information to the reader for a more complete understanding of the subject.

1. The book

Where does the idea of writing this book come from?

The book was not a result of the author's initiative. It was initially suggested and afterwards insisted upon by the Entities which incorporated the medium João. Consequently, writing about the subject was not a challenge but rather a mission. The author actually questioned the Entity on the reason for designating him to write such a book and was told that it was a mission which he should fulfill in the best possible way and which included making possible reference to ascendants linked to Spiritism.

Why is the book entitled Spiritual Cures?

The title seemed temporarily adequate to the author. As work progressed the title became definitive because it suited the intended purpose. It was not a chosen title, it came into being naturally. *Spiritual Cures* approaches the subject widely and without religious connotation, which would fatally occur had the title *Spiritist Cures* been adopted. The title might have been *Unexplainable Cures*, *Mental Cures*, *Psychic Cures*, *Paranormal Cures*, *Psychological Cures*, *Spiritual Manifestations*, *Miraculous Cures*, *Mediumistic Cures*, *Invisible Cures*, *Cures by Spirits*, *Medicine of the Soul*, *Medicine of Spirits*, or another related title. However, the author considered *Spiritual Cures* most appropriate.

On the topic of spiritual healings there are several technical terms, under medical, religious, and judicial aspects. How was the book produced in relation to this technical terminology?

The author is neither a Portuguese language expert nor knowledgeable in refined vocabulary. Even so, he aimed at a clear discourse by the use of words known to the great public. As often as possible the author transcribed the very words used by the interviewees, even if they were terminologically inappropriate terms. Therefore, a great deal of what is written in this book may not please doctors, religious people, or jurists. Nevertheless, what the author wanted consisted of unsophisticated communication via the use of simple and clear language.

Did the production of this book follow previously established criteria?

As the author was not certain of how to develop this assignment he began registering several details at random. Without greater difficulties he chose the use of interviews with generic and specific questions on the present topics and the strategy of note-taking for subsequent writing. The formulated questions attempt to translate what people actually desire to know, in other words, the author tried to formulate questions that are usually made. This method was even employed in the form of a self-interview with the author asking himself questions and answering them.

Apart from having been directly interviewed by the author, the citizen João Teixeira de Faria was also interviewed when he was incorporated, which means to say that the Entities which used the "instrument" João de Deus were consulted on several points and offered the answers needed in order to solve doubts[1]. As far as the questions made to the medium João are concerned, answers were sometimes brief and sometimes detailed. Such questions and answers were submitted to his appreciation prior to the publication of this book, all of which he approved.

The author made personal observations and maintained useful dialogues with administrators, workers, assistants, Casa visitors, doctors, lawyers, magistrates, public prosecutors, police chiefs, and religion scholars. He was also invited to travel alongside the medium João even to foreign countries, and on such occasions he stood both as an observer and as an assistant in procedures.

Did the author know with which Entity he spoke to?

No. There never was any identification regarding the book.

What is the purpose of this book?

It is possible to say that this book has two objectives. The first is to try to bring awareness to Brazilian authorities involved with this subject and even to private organizations, regarding the need to carry out scientific studies in order to detect possible frauds in the healing procedures of Casa

---

[1] After one of the interviews with the spiritual medium João, at Casa de Dom Inácio, occasion in which several questions were formulated, attendance works began. The author was seated and concentrated when the spiritual medium João-in-Entity approached and placed a hand in the author's head, saying that many of the questions, with some difficulties of answers, had been answered by the Entities, not by the spiritual medium.

de Dom Inácio and, in the absence of such frauds, the need on the part of these authorities to acknowledge the existence of spiritual healing. Casa de Dom Inácio has already been a place of research, having been studied more often by foreign scientists than by Brazilian ones.

The second objective is to offer general information of this place and to make the Casa's existence known to the greatest number of people who may, in some form or other, receive spiritual benefits.

Does the approximation between science and religion also constitute an objective?

The approximation between science and religion is not an objective *per se* but rather a consequence, if scientific research on spiritual healing happens to occur. It is not possible to state that there exists an actual movement to approximate science and religion nowadays, but the existence of such a tendency is indeed undeniable, even without some sort of organization or project. What we see are individual and spontaneous initiatives, in distinct moments and places, devoid of personal intentions and synchronization of procedures, but which move in the same direction.

There still remains a considerable distance between sciences in general and religions[2], but this will surely die out.

If one considers a pyramid the various religions and sciences are currently at the same level, at the base of the pyramid. Spiritual healing – regardless of religion or even in the denial of a religion – and medicine will sooner or later find themselves at the top of the pyramid. If that is taken for granted, the more spiritual healing is scientifically researched, the lower the top of the pyramid will be. Albert Einstein's words on the subject are worth mentioning: "Science without religion is lame, religion without science is blind".[3]

The present book is only a drop in the ocean of the intention of uniting science and religion.

How is the book structured?

The book is structured in six chapters for a more comprehensive and accessible understanding, as follows:

---

[2] "Pattern is an eternal doubt in science, whereas in religion such eternal doubt is blind faith". In: MENCONI, Darlene. As Razões da Fé. *Isto É*, Rio de Janeiro, n. 1889, p. 103.

[3] Idem, p. 104.

Chapter I – Introduction. This chapter offers a general view of the entire book with the necessary explanations for a smooth and pleasant reading.

Chapter II – João de Deus. In order to offer the reader information about the medium João Teixeira de Faria, known as "João de Deus", several questions were made regarding details which people usually desire to know.

Chapter III – Casa de Dom Inácio. A general idea is given on what Casa de Dom Inácio is like, a home of spiritual healing that is open to all, regardless of their religion.

Chapter IV – Entities. Many explanations are offered on the Entities that attend the Casa. The author obtained direct information from the Entities themselves according to the given permissions, in the form of questions asked to the medium João when incorporated, as well as from published research studies and from interviews with several mediums.

Chapter V – Spiritual Cures. This chapter has the same title as the book and constitutes the book's central theme, offering questions and answers related to common doubts involving spiritual healing. A considerable number of cures performed at the Casa are presented as examples and the names and addresses of the benefited individuals are also given for anyone interested in contacting them.

Chapter VI – Spiritual Manifestations and Brazilian Law. The author attempted to record judicial aspects involving the various forms of communication with spirits which have been analyzed by the Judiciary in some form or another. Some superficial explanations are presented regarding the penal aspect in a straightforward way for those who are not familiar with Law. References are made on religious freedom, scholarly opinions, and Judiciary decisions on the subject in real cases.

What were the author's concerns when elaborating this book?

Once he was assigned the mission of writing this book the author had a few important measures in mind, which may be summarized as follows:

a) To avoid religious confrontation: the book does not have a religious nature. It registers facts, not doctrinary aspects that may impose points of view. Spiritual cures exist in every religion.

b) To avoid scientific confrontation: the author has no intention of stating absolute truths and no defense is made on the hypothesis of spiritual healing replacing Medicine. On the contrary, it is imperative that spiritual and medical cures be partners and, in order for that to happen, intensive scientific research is necessary;

c) To avoid judicial confrontation: Brazilian laws must be respected; when a given law is not effective, it must be changed, not infringed. According to the author, the Brazilian penal legislation is absolutely correct in typifying illegal practice of medicine, charlatanism, and healing as crimes. There is a considerable number of cons in Brazil in all religions, but there are also serious occurrences which are scientifically unexplainable. In a country with high rates of violent criminality there is no reason to impose the law on honest individuals who only seek to perform good actions. In this case, serious conduct should be permitted judicially.

It is worth mentioning that the author's concerns of avoiding religious, scientific, and judicial confrontation only follow the principles of Casa de Dom Inácio, which aim to avoid any type of confrontation whatsoever.

There was no hurry to conclude the production of this book, especially because of the fact that the author needed to solve several doubts on the subject. This was only possible through frequent visits to the Casa and observation of procedures performed there, as well as by reading several books on the topic.

What does the frequently mentioned expression "conventional medicine" mean?

It refers to the Medicine which is commonly known and practiced and which follows a set of accepted standards.

Does the book solely focus on Casa de Dom Inácio?

It was suggested that the book should present how the Casa operates and the spiritual cures performed there. The central idea is that reports of what happens at the Casa serve as comparison for what occurs in other locations. Regardless of religious belief, spiritual cures do exist.

What message does the book cover aim to convey?

None, it only aims to reveal the location of Casa de Dom Inácio. On the front cover there is a world map with Goiás State's geographical position and on the back cover a map of Goiás situates Abadiânia, Brasília, Anápolis, and Goiânia. Both covers attempt to serve as a guide to anyone intending to go to Casa de Dom Inácio.

Would it be possible for the book to be published and sold by the Casa without the mediation of a publishing company?

Yes. The publication could be independent, which would result in lower sale prices and difficulties in distribution. Therefore, the author preferred to publish the book via a publishing house, which makes the book more expensive but allows for a wider and easier distribution.

Was it difficult to write this book?

Yes, but it was a rewarding job. As the author wrote about a subject which was almost entirely unknown to him, the work demanded keen observation and several interviews. In addition, the author had to read and research a great deal.

Does the author intend to profit with this book?

No. There was a great number of people involved in the production of this book. Therefore, the author prefers to confer the copyright for Casa de Dom Inácio, where it will be of valuable use.

No financial advantages may surpass the spiritual benefits received by the author through this book.

Are there individuals who profit with books or other activities by using the Casa and the medium João?

Yes, and such exclusive consideration for economic aspects that relegates spiritual matters to a secondary position cannot be a good thing. There are books, photographs, and documentaries which are commercialized without any control or participation of the Casa in the obtained profit.

It is possible to say that mankind is constantly anguished in search of the true meaning of life. Does the book approach this topic in any way?

The author does not feel sufficiently confident to write about certain topics. There are good books written by competent people that approach the spiritual subject more effectively.

Fight for survival, planned projects, and daily routine greatly reduce existential questions. Regardless of religious beliefs, nationality, sex, cultural background, or socioeconomic situation, every person has moments of existential reflection in which he/she questions the meaning of life. Human beings have always sought this meaning and will always do so.[4] One only needs to look up at the stars, observe the perfection of the "machinery" of the human body, and contemplate nature in order to ask that most universal of questions: "Who am I, where did I come from, and where am I going?"

Chico Xavier is mentioned in several passages of this book. Who was he?

Francisco Cândido Xavier (Chico Xavier) was born on July 2, 1910, in Pedro Leopoldo, Minas Gerais. A son of João Cândido Xavier and Maria João de Deus, he was orphaned by his mother's death at the age of 5 and was placed under the care of his godmother Rita de Cássia, with whom he suffered considerably in what later became ostensive ill-treatment. His other eight brothers and sisters were also distributed to various relatives and friends.

When his widowed father married Adélia Batista, who insisted on reuniting all of João Cândido's children, Chico had a second mother. From his father's second marriage Chico Xavier had six more brothers and sisters, totaling 14, with whom he lived during 10 years of peace and harmony, together with his father and his new mother. Chico received permanent protection from his real mother, Maria João de Deus, from the age of 5 to 17, through his constant contact with her in spiritual visions. In such visions he talked to her and obtained advice on how to behave, which he rigorously followed.

His mediumship was revealed when he was 4 years old, for he saw and heard spirits and spoke to them. To him there was no difference between the material and the spiritual world. At the age of 8 he began working in order to help his family. He worked in a fabric factory and later as a wiring worker, a grocery store assistant, and an agricultural inspector, before retiring as a typist after several years of intense activity. Chico never mixed up his professional activities with his mediumship.

As far as his eye illness was concerned, he had a dislocation of the crystalline lens as well as squint on his right eye which disturbed him day

---

[4] "The true meaning of life is love. Love is a state of mind of unconditional donation which imposes upon us the duty of thinking about the other's afflictions as well". In: MAES, Hercílio, *Mediunidade de Cura*, p. 168.

and night. His visual problem was later aggravated by cataract which inflicted severe pain on him. Chico refused Zé Arigó's offer to perform a spiritual surgery in his eyes with the argument that the illness was a trial and, therefore, he had to bear it.

It is important to mention that in 1939, with the death of his brother José Cândido Xavier, Chico took up the guardianship of his nephews and his brother's widow Geni. His deceased brother had left an electricity bill that was impossible to pay with Chico's small income. One day he was visited by a stranger, who said he had come to pay a previously acquired debt. He then presented an envelope before leaving which, when opened, contained the exact amount needed to pay the debt of Chico's deceased brother.

Before definitively adopting Spiritism, Chico sought help in Catholicism, his initial religion, from which he parted because it did not offer explanations for the phenomena he witnessed. The priest who listened to his confessions and offered him guidance for the path he sought gave him his blessings instead of attempting to dissuade him. He was more than a friend to Chico, he was a true father.

Chico's first psychographed book was *Parnaso de Além-Túmulo* (Parnassus Beyond the Grave) in 1932, a collection of poems which caused great impact in Brazil's cultural stage and resulted in intense polemic due to the fact that it was produced by famous dead poets (Casimiro de Abreu, Castro Alves, Olavo Bilac, Augusto dos Anjos, Antônio Nobre, Alphonsus Guimarães, Antero de Quental, Guerra Junqueiro, D. Pedro II, and others). The style resembled that of these writers when they were alive, a phenomenon which failed to be explained.

At the beginning of his mediumistic work, the raised controversies served to make Spiritism and the young medium well-known. Chico Xavier possessed exceptional mediumship, for he revealed not only clairvoyance, clairaudience, and physical effects, but an extraordinary psychographic ability as well.

Chico Xavier lived moments of extreme apprehension: for instance, he was sued together with the Brazilian Spiritist Federation by the family of Humberto de Campos, who wanted to attest the truth of the authorship of the psychographed books which were allegedly dictated by the spirit Humberto de Campos. But it all ended happily.[5]

As psychographed books increased in number, Xavier's fame and stories regarding his powers as a medium grew likewise. This brought

---

[5] Further details on this lawsuit are revealed in Chapter VI, n. 14.

Chico serious concerns which often led him to make public announcements of his inability to make the blind see or the paralytic walk.

Xavier served as an instrument for several spirits, among them André Luiz and Bezerra de Menezes, but his spiritual mentor was Emmanuel.[6] At the beginning of Emmanuel's contacts with Chico Xavier – later it was agreed that they would work together for a long time – the good spirit imposed three basic principles to be followed by the medium: first, discipline; second, discipline; and third, discipline. Furthermore, Emmanuel stated that, should he offer advice not in accordance with the teachings of Jesus and Kardec, Chico should remain with them and seek to forget Emmanuel.

Throughout his life he psychographed poetry, novels, novellas, short stories, chronicles, reports, messages, General History, religion, Sociology, Philosophy, and children's literature, totaling 412 books, with thousands of publications translated into English, French, Castellan, Esperanto, Japanese, Greek etc. His copyrights were donated to philanthropic institutions. Chico always lived on a modest retirement pension.

Psychographic work was not only simple mediumistic concentration but also a tiring physical activity that demanded complete dedication and reduced sleeping hours. Chico's health was always debilitating and required permanent medical care. His mediumship did not offer him any personal privileges. According to him, it was thanks to medical recommendation that he moved from Pedro Leopoldo to Uberaba at the age of 48, where he resided until his death. Chico once remarked that "Pedro Leopoldo is my birth place and Uberaba is my blessing". He traveled throughout Brazil and visited the United States, England, France, Italy, and Portugal in service of the Spiritist doctrine.

His humbleness and charity inspired countless people and resulted in hospitals, orphanages, crèches, homes for the disabled, soup for the poor, food campaigns, medical ambulatories, adult literacy, libraries etc. If there existed a hierarchy in Spiritism similar to that in Catholicism, Chico Xavier might be considered the "Pope of Spiritism".

His vast psychographed work include: *Parnaso de Além-Túmulo*; *Cartas de uma Morta* (Letters of a Dead Woman); *Brasil, Coração do Mundo, Pátria do Evangelho* (Brazil, Heart of the World, Nation of Gospels); *A Caminho da Luz* (*Towards the Light*)[*]; *Há 2000 Anos*

---

[6] Further information on Emmanuel are revealed in Chapter IV, n. 6.

[*] Books with titles in italic were translated into English. – T.N.

(*2000 Years Ago*); *50 Anos Depois* (50 Years Later); *O Consolador* (The Consoling One); *Boa Nova* (Good News); *Paulo e Estevão* (Paul and Stephan); *Nosso Lar* (translated into English as *The Astral City*); *Os Mensageiros* (The Messengers); *Obreiros da Vida Eterna* (Workers of Eternal Life); *Voltei* (I have returned); *Entre a Terra e o Céu* (Between Earth and Sky); *Evolução em Dois Mundos* (Evolution in Two Worlds); *Mecanismos de Mediunidade* (Mechanisms of Mediumship); and *Desobsessão* (*Disobsession*).

Chico Xavier died on June 30, 2002 at the age of 92, 75 of which were dedicated to the communication between the living and the dead.

Do all of Chico Xavier's deeds deserve credibility?

Yes. In certain situations even those who do not believe respect the facts. This indeed happens in relation to Chico Xavier. No one in their right minds questions his psychographic mediumship. It would be humanly impossible to gather so much information concerning his intellectual production: he wrote more than 400 books on various subjects. He revealed himself to be at the same time a chronicler, a novelist, a poet, a prose writer, a historian, a sociologist, and a philosopher.

2. Absence of religious confrontation

Is it not a religious confrontation to admit spiritual healing?

No, because spiritual healing occur in all religions. Whether one's faith is religious or merely positive thinking, it is up to each person to decide. Regardless of religion there have been quite a few reports that a person was completely cured. It does not matter how God is named because faith in a higher power is typical of every religion. What differs are the paths chosen.

Spiritual cures motivated by faith or by positive thinking are not questioned, defended, or attacked in this book. The aim is to register cases that are considered scientifically unexplainable.

Is it important to have faith?

Yes, faith is extremely important in the search for cure even in conventional medical treatments.

Are there any differences between faith and religion?

Yes, in the author's opinion. Religion – with its various names – is a human creation, therefore it has merits and flaws. Faith is an inner feeling that is inherent to all human beings, regardless of their religion.

It has been stated that Casa de Dom Inácio is not a Spiritist center. Nevertheless, are not the procedures performed there in tune with the Spiritist doctrine?

To a certain extent, yes, but the Casa does not impose restrictions on any religious creed. The majority of people who visit the Casa call themselves Catholics, as does the medium João. Any chant from any given religion in any language may be sung by a group of people.

Several mass celebrations and cults have been conducted by priests and Protestant clergymen at the Casa. During the evenings people pray the rosary and on Sunday mornings there are meditation sessions with fraternal and universal prayers in many languages, with no specific religious nature.

Apart from worshippers of the so-called Christian religions, Buddhists, Hinduists, and Muslims are also welcome at the Casa, as well as people known to be materialists.

How were mass celebrations conducted at Casa de Dom Inácio?

More than once, a priest who was a member of an American travel group asked for permission to perform mass there.

Is it common for religious authorities to visit the Casa?

No, it is not. However, visits do occur sometimes, often motivated by curiosity. An American Protestant bishop, PhD in Religion, attended the Casa for two weeks and was deeply impressed with what he saw. Something similar happened to a Protestant clergyman who was taken by the author to see the Casa and witness the procedures performed there.

Is it good for a person simply to attend religious temples (of any religion)?

Yes, because the simple fact of being close to other people who have the best intentions by going there already produces spiritual benefits. However, positive results may be even better if there is spiritual surrender as well as physical presence.

3. Absence of scientific confrontation

Is there no confrontation as far as Medicine is concerned?

No. It is widely known that Medicine is not an exact science and that unpredictable facts may occur and elude all kinds of scientific explanation.

Spiritual cures are regarded by conventional medicine as occurrences devoid of scientific explanation. Those who truly believe in or perform spiritual healing are defenders of Medicine.

Therefore, Medicine and spiritual healing are not rivals. Any kind of confrontation between them indicates simple-mindedness and lack of scientific view. Spiritual healing is not an alternative for conventional medicine because both should be united, not confronted. A doctor cures the body, but the sick needs to be guided in a moral transformation. The latter is achieved by spiritual healing. Medicine deserves the utmost respect and incentive from those who believe in spiritual healing. All those who have a mission to serve as an instrument for spiritual healing believe in Medicine, they have sought it and will continue to do so.

The medium is only the channel of communication between the physical and the spiritual worlds. Spiritual healing only proves that there is life after death and that good spirits may offer solutions which human medicine is unable to present in some cases.

In Casa de Dom Inácio's specific case, do the cures performed there confront Medicine?

No, cures performed at the Casa in no way intend to confront Medicine, so much so that there is explicit and repeated recommendation not to abandon medical treatment. The medication prescribed by the Entities does not have any contraindication.

Does not the simple acceptance of spiritual healing characterize confrontation with conventional medicine?

Absolutely not. Spiritual healing and sciences in general have the same goal, the physical and spiritual welfare of human beings in the search of spiritual peace. Spiritual treatment does not exclude medical treatment, they complete each other.

Is there a competition between the service provided at Casa de Dom Inácio and that of medical professionals? In other words, from a commercial point of view, is the Casa taking clients away from doctors?

Spiritual healing performed at Casa de Dom Inácio is done so in those cases in which conventional medicine is yet unable to carry out an effective treatment or when an individual does not have financial income to pay for medical expenses. The number of services which only result in spiritual peace and of people who are recommended to a doctor by the Entity is considerable. In other cases, service allows for partial healing and the Entity recommends the aid of conventional medicine for the conclusion of treatments.

How does a doctor offer continuity to a spiritual treatment?

There are many cases in which the doctor tells the patient that his/her health problem is progressive and that nothing can be done about it. Once spiritual healing is performed and the patient returns for a medical appointment, the doctor finds out that the problem has been paralyzed. Some believe in the patient's report, others do not. They admit that something unexplainable happened and that permanent monitoring must be made in order to avoid recurrence.[7]

Does conventional medicine advance and gradually obtain cures for previously incurable illnesses?

Yes, and it always will. Progress is a result of the hard work of professionals who are truly enlightened spirits with the mission of working for the benefit of humankind. These persistent researchers promote discoveries or inventions[8] that will benefit many people in the future. Nevertheless, spiritual medicine is different from conventional medicine.

How is that justified?

There is nothing to be justified. What is unknown nowadays will be no surprise in the future. This is humankind's natural progress. Anesthesia and some vaccines, for instance, are relatively recent.

Are doctors radically against spiritual healing?

Not all of them. A considerable number believes in something which science cannot explain. Doctors are not different from ordinary citizens: they have families and religions and are members in a given social and cultural context. They underwent scientific training in order to perform the noble mission of caring for human beings. They deserve the utmost respect and admiration for their

---

[7] Recurrence is a medical term which indicates that an illness or a symptom has returned after a reasonably long period of cure.

[8] Discovery: to find something that exists, but which was unknown.

Invention: creation of something which did not exist.

chosen profession. It is natural that they should focus more on science than on spiritual matters.

Is there some form of organization of doctors who believe in spiritual healing?

Associação Médico-Espírita (AME, Spiritist-Medical Association) has regional offices in several states and includes not only doctors but other professionals from Medicine-related areas: nurses, psychologists, nutritionists, pharmacists, therapists etc. As far as the author knows, according to the AME spiritual treatment is a complement of conventional medical treatment.

Could spiritual healing be nothing but the result of positive thinking or powers which certain "sensitive" or "paranormal" individuals possess and which are explained by the science of Parapsychology?

Indeed, under certain aspects, it is possible to state that fluidified water and certain medications administered in cures would equate to placebos in medicine, which are completely harmless to an organism but reveal positive results in the simple fact that a person believes in the power of cure.

Without doubt, positive thinking is an important factor in spiritual healing, but it is not the only one. Spiritual intervention, unexplainable by science, makes even a non-believer's cure possible. Scientifically, Parapsychology attempts to offer explanations. To accept or not arguments on the subject is controversial and the author does not have sufficient knowledge for such a discussion.

4. Absence of juridical confrontation

Does spiritual healing performed at Casa de Dom Inácio characterize juridical confrontation?

No, spiritual healing performed at the Casa does not constitute crimes in the terms discussed in this book. If one takes into account that real-life cases do not have a scientific explanation and that procedures employed there are constitutionally protected by religious freedom, then conducts are licit.

Does the sale of medication, such as Passiflora, characterize an illegal practice of pharmaceutical activity?

No, simply selling it does not constitute a crime. Illicit conduct refers to performing a given profession without legal authorization. At Casa de Dom Inácio

Passiflora is legally prepared by a pharmacist registered in the Regional Pharmacy Council. The preparation and wrapping follow legal guidelines.

Is there a predisposition on the part of the Judiciary against spiritual healing?

Not at all. Normally, if there is some sort of predisposition, it is in favor of spiritual healing, regardless of religious creed.

Magistrates apply the law, they do not make them. If illegal medical practice, charlatanism, and healing are typified as crimes and if a criminal lawsuit has collected unfavorable evidence against the accused, magistrates are not able to decide against the law. It is for this exact reason that one must make clear what is fraud and what is truth – albeit unexplainable to science – so the Judiciary may decide on the non-existence of crime.

Does the author mean to say that Brazilian magistrates believe in spiritual healing?

Not all of them do. A judge is an ordinary citizen with a degree in Law who passed a public exam and who performs the noble and difficult task of judging. The religious beliefs of judges are not different from those of other people. There is a spontaneous belief in the population at large in life after death and such movement similarly occurs among magistrates.

Is there some sort of organization of magistrates who believe in life after death and, consequently, in spiritual healing?

Yes. Associação Brasileira dos Magistrados Espíritas (ABRAME, Brazilian Association of Spiritist Magistrates) is similar to Associação Médico-Espírita Brasileira (AME), whose noble principle is the spiritualization of Justice and the humanization of the Judiciary.

5. Medium and mediumship

What is a medium?

As a simple explanation for non-experts on the subject, a medium is a person who acts as a mediator in the communication with spirits. In addition, mediumship may be understood as the human ability of establishing links with the spiritual world.[9]

---

[9] PIRES, J. Herculano. *Arigó* – Vida, mediunidade e martírio, p. 19.

How can mediums be classified?

There are several forms of classification. It is not this book's aim to present a complete or thorough classification; instead a basic classification is presented in order to be understood by non-experts on the subject.

Mediums may be classified as:

- mediums of physical effects (they move objects, produce noises etc.);
- speakers (spirits speak through them);
- seers (they see);
- hearers (they hear);
- intuitive (they capture thoughts);
- inspired (they receive thoughts as suggestions);
- psychographers (they write);
- healers (they serve as instruments for spirits to promote cures).

Healing mediums, as a rule, may cure sick people through passes and prayers. Healing mediums who work via physical contact are rare.

How is mediumship explained?

The teachings of an expert on the subject are much more effective than the author's own attempt at explanation:[10]

At birth, a person possesses five senses: touch, smell, hearing, sight, and taste. With them and through them a person relates with nature, with other living beings, and with material things. Such contact is processed in a narrow vibrating strip, because our senses are limited.

Apart from these five senses, a person comes into the world with a sixth sense, called the extra-sensorial sense or simply mediumship. It is a faculty in our organism which allows us to interact with the immaterial world that has often been interpreted as supernatural. In some people the sixth sense is enhanced to such a degree that it penetrates in dimensions that are beyond the limits of the five senses and the instruments of official science.

People who have an enhanced sixth sense are called sensitive, paranormal, or mediums.

---

[10] GODINHO, Javier. In: *Revista Espírita Allan Kardec*. Ano XIII, n. 53, p. 3.

Is a medium a different person?

No, a medium is as ordinary as everybody else. The poem dictated to Chico Xavier by the spirit Jair Presente is revealing:

A MEDIUM

What is in fact a medium?
This mischievous question
Shows that you have
Lots of doubts in your head.
A medium is a person
Who works, struggles, and feels
Cheers up, suffers, and cries
As we all do.
He has crazy heart beats,
Bladder disorder,
Kidney pains, urine incontinence,
Weakness and stomachache...
With a delicate stomach,
He often feels heartburn,
Complicated gall bladder,
Nausea and dysentery.
Whenever he eats too much
From the plates in his hand
He gets afflicted and indisposed
Or moans of indigestion.
He has fever and headache
When he catches cold.
His nerves are wild and crazy
Almost all the time.
In love he has sympathies
As is true of everyone
If it is she, she thinks of a man
If it is he, he thinks of a woman.
He needs, in this respect,
Instruction and doctrine,
For love, in
Any speck of time,
Does not dismiss discipline.
If you want to be a medium,
Keep the faith that never falls,
Hold on to Jesus Christ,
Learn to serve and go about...[11]

Do the incorporated medium João and the Entity share the same meaning?

They may not have a common meaning in a more thorough analysis concerning religious and scientific aspects for those with greater knowledge on the subject. However, in this book which is only a personal report and is devoid of any religious or scientific discussion, both the incorporated medium João and the Entity share the same meaning.

---

[11] *Revista Universo Espírita*, ano 2, n. 24, p. 19.

If the medium João receives several spirits, would it not be more logical to refer to "Entities" (in the plural) rather than to an "Entity" (in the singular), as can be seen throughout this book?

There are indeed many references to "Entities" in this book because there are many which use the "instrument" that is João de Deus. Although some of them may be identified by people who attend the Casa regularly, the generic term "Entity", in the singular form, has been chosen to designate all the "Entities", and there is no concern over which Entity is using the medium João as an "instrument" in any given moment.

Is the author a medium?

Yes, in a way, for every person is a medium to a greater or lesser degree.

What kind of medium is the author?

By excluding the medium of physical effects, the seer, the hearer, the intuitive, the psychographer, and the healer, the author classifies himself as an inspired medium.

Based on what evidence does the author identify himself as an inspired medium?

On the very elaboration of this book. At the beginning, the author had not the slightest idea of what he should write. However, the ideas appeared naturally.

6. Commenting on spiritual cures

Did the author witness or notice many spiritual cures?

Yes, hundreds of spiritual surgeries were witnessed and hundreds of cures were perceived in conversations with benefited individuals, many of which excited special attention. However, instead of reporting what he witnessed, the author preferred to report some real-life stories of people who were spiritually cured.[12]

What if the reader does not believe in spiritual cures?

Not for a single moment was the author concerned with whether the reader would believe this report or not. There is no commercial objective or

---

[12] See Chapter V, n. 18.

religious intention. A few will believe, many will not, and a considerable number will remain in doubt.

It is opportune to quote Saint Ignatius' manifestation on the subject: "For those who believe, no words are necessary; for those who do not believe, no words are possible."

How can one believe in what he/she does not see?

There are those who believe without seeing, those who do not believe even when witnessing impossible surgeries from the perspective of conventional medicine, and those who see and doubt.

There are people who reach certain conclusions by the guidance of faith and love and others who reach this inner peace only through pain. For those who believe, nothing more than the confirmation of their belief will occur; for those who do not believe, what remains is the author's respect for such attitude; and for those who doubt, may they try to solve their doubts.

Do you mean that doubt should be respected?

Yes. Doubt should be respected just as belief should be. The benefit of the doubt is given to anyone who wants to reflect upon facts, people, life, and and to anyone who does more than merely accept things as they are without questioning. Even if one's attitude reveals conformism it must be well grounded, it must be the result of some consideration, of a conscientious decision.

Is the attempt of convincing people who do not believe in spiritual healing valid?

The book does not aim to convince anybody, only to report facts. To believe or not to believe is a personal choice. It is up to the reader to observe, read, and inquire benefited individuals in order to reach an honest and sincere conclusion. The truth depends on a person's private search.

It is widely thought that a person who does not share anxieties, sorrow, traumas, disappointments, complexes, feelings of guilt, and other problems may eventually suffer from psychic illnesses. Should this kind of person start sharing such problems?

Yes, and any form of communication is acceptable in order for the person to show what he/she feels. In the author's opinion the sharing of feelings with a priest (confession), clergyman, psychologist, relative, or even a friend will always result in benefits for both the body and the soul.

7. Other information

Which is prone to illness, the body or the spirit?

The spirit, because the body is nothing more than the material exterior. The cause lies in the spirit but the effect is shown in the body.

What causes an illness?

There are various causes. Every negative thought and conduct may produce illnesses. In addition, the notorious "deadly sins" may also result in body illnesses: wrath, lust, gluttony, sloth, pride, greed, and envy.

Are good companies important?

Yes, being close to altruistic people produces positive fluids. On the other hand, proximity to individuals with a negative conduct may only result in negative fluids. Therefore one should always look for good company.

Is the act of almsgiving considered charity?

Not always. Almsgiving may be a strictly mechanical gesture and charity is much more than that. True charity is also moral in nature and refers to love in its entirety, a love which is felt for all human beings.

Does almsgiving result in benefits for those who give?

According to the author it depends on the situation at hand. Alms which is given "mechanically" does not mean very much because what matters most is the quality of what is given, not the quantity. In certain situations a donation of words may be more positive for those who receive it than a material donation. For the donator, regardless of what is given, the intention is more important than the act.

What does "death" mean?

There is no life or death. What occurs is nothing more than the loss of the "material exterior" which is the human body. The spirit, be it incarnate or not, is always alive. Life is not restricted to this short period of time between the cradle and the grave.[13] A dead body is proof of the soul's existence. One should not look for the soul where it is not. The so-called death of the physical body is the preparation for eternal life.

---

[13] SILVA, José Antônio Ferreira da. A Paz começa em mim. *Revista Universo Espírita*, 2nd year, n. 26, p. 30.

What does "the end of the world" mean?

This is another subject which the author does not feel confident enough to comment on. According to public knowledge, the end of the world constitutes the disappearance of the planet Earth, of the solar system, or of our galaxy (Milky Way). However, it will never constitute the end of the Universe, which is infinite.

Here is how the end of the planet Earth might occur from a scientific point of view:

In a few billion years' time (from 1 to 5, depending on who's counting), the Milky Way will crash into neighboring galaxy M-31, better known as Andromeda. As stars stand at a considerable distance from each other the collision will not affect the solar system. Nevertheless it would be a beautiful sight: the sky would have more stars, with two white stripes at night instead of one. It is a pity that there will probably not be anyone alive around here to observe the spectacle.

The last thing that anyone would wish to be 7 billion years from now is an insurance agent, because then the Sun will swell a great deal beyond its diameter and will vaporize everything within its reach, including Earth. It will not be a pretty sight to see the planet leave its orbit, dragged by the gravity of a Sun with millions of kilometers in diameter, and burn at 100,000 degrees Celsius. The only thing that will remain will be individual atoms from Earth, launched back into space.

Fortunately nobody will be around to witness the scene. Earth will have become inhabitable long before this happens. 500 million years from now all kinds of complex life will probably have disappeared, according to some scientists, that is, if nothing else occurs before this. There is always the possibility of an asteroid crashing down on our heads. It is estimated that every 100 million years Earth is hit by a meteor of the same dimensions of the one which exterminated dinosaurs. The last of such meteors hit Earth 65 million years ago. (HOLTZ)

One of the greatest difficulties of accepting the spiritual world is the need to understand the meaning of infinity, a concept related to the size of the universe. Is it possible to summarize its meaning?

The notion of infinity must be approached by both religious and scientific angles at the same time.

As far as the religious angle is concerned there is no better source than the teachings of Allan Kardec on the present subject which are hereby transcribed. The following excerpt is extracted from the Spirits' Book, Chapter One (God and Infinity), questions 2 and 3.

What is to be understood by Infinity?

"That which has neither beginning nor end; the unknown: all that is unknown is infinite."

Can it be said that God is infinity?

"An incomplete definition. Poverty of human speech incompetent to define what transcends human intelligence."

God is infinite in His perfections, but "infinity" is an abstraction. To say that God is infinity is to substitute the attribute of a thing for the thing itself, and to define something unknown by reference to some other thing equally unknown.[14]

From a scientific point of view, the following extract is worth quoting in order to present the notion of distance:

It's natural to think the stars and planets are much closer than they really are – after all, in everyday life we have no experience of the huge distances of space. Those distances are so large that it doesn't even make sense to measure them in feet or miles, the way we measure most lengths. Instead we use the light-year, which is the distance light travels in a year. In one second, a beam of light will travel 186,000 miles, so a light-year is a very long distance…

… the nearest star, Proxima Centauri, is about four light-years, or twenty-three million million miles, away. Most of the other stars that are visible to the naked eye lie within a few hundred light-years of us. Our sun, for comparison, is a mere eight light-minutes away! The visible stars appear spread all over the night sky but are particularly concentrated in one band, which we call the Milky Way…[16]

---

[14] KARDEC, Allan. *The Spirits' Book*. Trans. Anna Blackwell. 10 ed. São Paulo: LAKE, 2003. p. 63.

[15] Also known as Alpha Centauri C.

[16] The Milky Way itself is but one of more than a hundred billion galaxies that can be seen using modern telescopes – and each galaxy contains on average some one hundred billion stars. If a star were a grain of salt, you could fit all the stars visible to the naked eye on a teaspoon, but all the stars in the universe would fill a ball more than eight miles wile. HAWKING, Stephen *et.al.* In: *A Briefer History of Time*. p. 53.

... the Milky Way – our galaxy – is about one hundred thousand light-years across and is slowly rotating; the stars in its spiral arms orbit around its center about once every several hundred million years. Our sun is just an ordinary, average-sized yellow star near the inner edge of one of the spiral arms. (IIAWKING)

Still on the topic of distance, the author hereby makes use of English astronomer Sir James Jeans' enlightening reflections on the magnitude of our galaxy and adapts them slightly for a more effective understanding. Let us imagine the Sun, a star of fifth magnitude, which would correspond to seven parts of 1 millimeter divided into a thousand equal parts – therefore, something invisible to the naked eye. The Earth's orbit around the Sun would correspond to ½ (half) a millimeter and would be visible to one with perfect eyesight. Our solar system would correspond to approximately 2 centimeters. In such a comparison, the Milky Way would equate to 20,000 kilometers. Therefore, the solar system would amount to the same 2 centimeters located along the 20,000 kilometers. A spaceship traveling at light speed would take about 50,000 light-years to travel from Earth to the extremity of the Milky Way.[17]

If one admits that all the procedures at Casa de Dom Inácio constitute serious practice, is there not alleged healing in other locations?

Yes. There are cons, frauds, simulations, and other forms of exploitation of people's beliefs regarding spiritual healing. One must separate what is serious from what constitutes fantasy, even if these are occasionally devoid of bad intentions.

The practices described here are also applicable in other serious institutions, regardless of religious creed.

Is Casa de Dom Inácio worth visiting?

Yes, the Casa is worth visiting whether one believes or not, or has doubts.

Why the name "João de Deus" ("John of God")?

This name is used in several passages of this book. It is not an act of pretension on the medium João's part, but the stating of a fact: visitors at Casa de Dom Inácio affectionately refer to him as "João de Deus".

---

[17] FRANCO, Divaldo P. *No Limiar do Infinito*, p. 22/23.

Chapter II

João de Deus

João Teixeira de Faria, known as João de Deus ("John of God"), is both special and ordinary. He is special because of his mediumistic gift and ordinary because he possesses all the virtues and flaws, qualities and imperfections, which are typical of human beings.

To many he may be considered sensitive or paranormal. His mediumistic gift is undeniable. João spiritually understands that he has a 'mission' and intends to fulfill it in the best possible way.

1. Family

What is your name?

João Teixeira de Faria.

When were you born?

June 24, 1942.

Where were you born?

I was born in Cachoeira da Fumaça, present-day Cachoeira de Goiás, where I lived until the age of 3.

What are your parents' names?

José Nunes de Faria (Juca) and Francisca Teixeira Damas (Iuca), both deceased. He was a tailor and she was a housewife.

How many brothers do you have?

Five brothers, I am the youngest.

Where did you spend your childhood?

In Itapaci, Goiânia, and Anápolis, but especially in Itapaci, a town located close to the Belém-Brasília highway and approximately 220 km from Abadiânia.

How can you describe your childhood and adolescence?

My parents were always very poor, so I had to start work at a very young age in order to help with family expenses. I left home to work at the age of 14.

How would you describe your life, marriage, children, family, and friends?

I am an ordinary man like any other.

How many children do you have?

Nine children.

2. Ordinary citizen

Is it difficult to balance the citizen's routine with that of the medium?

I am already used to it and I always attempt to balance both as best as I can.

Are there great difficulties in being an ordinary citizen, going to a restaurant, sitting with friends in a bar, and talking at leisure?

I am not very fond of going out. When I have some free time I prefer going to the farm.

What is your formal education level?

I studied for three months but I was expelled from school due to lack of payment.

How did this happen?

It was a private school and I used to pay expenses by filling the school's big water tank. There was no electricity at the time, so the water tank was filled with the use of a pump with a hand lever. I used to start pumping water at five in the morning, alternating the pumping with both hands. By 7 am the tank was full and I could go to classes.

The school was sold and the new owners did not allow me to continue paying the school through services. My parents were extremely poor and could not afford to pay the school. As a result I was forbidden to attend it.

Does the fact of not having studied cause you any problems as a citizen?
No, not at all.

What jobs have you had?

I have worked as an assistant stonemason, a brickmaker, a cistern worker, a dry cleaner, a tailor, and a prospector, among others.

It is a popular opinion that João Teixeira de Faria may be regarded as a rich person because of his considerable material patrimony. Is this not incompatible with mediumship?

I am not rich, but I do have a patrimony which allows me to live with dignity. Besides, a material patrimony has nothing to do with mediumship.

Do you have any spare time for your private affairs, especially concerning the financial aspect, considering your intense dedication to mediumship?

I always try to organize procedures in order to have more time for my private affairs.

Would it be economically viable for you to stop working and dedicate solely to mediumistic activities?

Material possessions do not resist a confrontation with spiritual possessions. My economic situation is currently stable, but I have suffered from hunger in the past. I know what poverty is like. My present routine – which involves three days for the practice of good, three days for my private affairs, and one day for rest – is satisfactory.

Do you contribute financially for the maintenance of Casa de Dom Inácio?

Whenever there are any expenses and the Casa does not have any money, I pay them.

Do you feel anxieties?
Sometimes.

Why do you feel anxieties if you are aware of your good deeds?

I am an ordinary person but I am very sensitive. Small problems affect me greatly.

Have you ever been involved in party politics?

As far as putting myself up for candidacy, never. My electoral constituency is in Abadiânia. I treat all politicians well and they treat me in the same way. I am a personal friend of many of them. As a citizen and a voter, I have my political preferences.

It is said that you were a victim of several injustices and groundless accusations. Can you comment on this?

It is true, I was a victim of many injustices, but to comment on them means suffering all over again. I prefer to forget everything. What had to happen did.

Have you ever been sick and in need of medical assistance?

I constantly need doctors. Spiritual healing is not incompatible with human medicine. I go to the dentist on a regular basis and I have health problems like any normal person.[18] I do not have any problems with being submitted to exams and taking medication prescribed by doctors. When I am not incorporated I am an ordinary person.

According to all that has been said, can one state that you, as a medium, do not have privileges but personal sacrifices instead?

Yes, I have no privileges. Mediumship does not offer benefits to anyone, it is a divine mission and must be fulfilled.[19]

You have a long-standing group of followers. Can doctors be found among them?

Yes, several doctors have been following me for many years.

Do you have any nicknames?

When I was a child I was known as "João da Iuca" ("Iuca's John), because of my mother's nickname. I was also known as "João Curador" ("Healing John") in other locations. At the beginning of my activities in Abadiânia I started being called "João de Abadiânia" ("John of Abadiânia"). Nowadays I am affectionately called "João de Deus".

Why the name "João de Deus" ("John of God")?

I am not able to explain exactly the reason for this nickname or when it first appeared. I believe it has to do with the spiritual cures performed by various Entities which use me simply as an "apparatus".

---

[18] One episode deserves to be mentioned. A friend of João and doctor paid him a home visit one day. When he arrived there he said he had just gone to see how João was, but he ended up taking the latter's pressure. The doctor was alarmed with the result and immediately took him to a hospital and had him admitted in order to receive medical care for a few days. On the following day, the medium João said he would leave the hospital no matter what happened because he had to attend people from several parts of the world. He left the hospital and went to Abadiânia.

The author went after him on that very day in order to discuss juridical problems. The medium told him that his physical condition was not good for such a discussion and that the author should attempt to solve the matter in the best possible way. João then saw the people present and later returned home in a clearly fragile physical condition.

[19] During one of the trips alongside the author, the medium João said he was in great need of a check-up on his health but did not have time to do it because his priority consisted in seeing those who sought his help.

3. Wanderings

In which cities have you lived, even during short periods?

I have lived in many cities, which include Colinas (TO), Pilar (GO), Crixás (GO), Presidente Kennedy (TO), Guaraí (TO), Barreiras (BA), Canabrava (BA), Imperatriz (MA), Tocantinópolis (TO), Vila Rondom (PA), Belém (PA), Tucuruí (PA), Maceió (AL), Niterói (RJ), Campo Grande (MT), Brasília (DF), Campos Belos (GO), Santo Ângelo (RS), Goiânia (GO), and Anápolis (GO), where I now live.

It seems you have wandered a great deal before settling in Abadiânia, is this true?

Yes, it is, I have always been restless. I was never completely satisfied in one place because something was always missing and I did not know what. I only became calm and satisfied when I started tending to the public in Abadiânia.

Why did you settle in Abadiânia?

In 1979 Decil de Sá Abreu[20], the then mayor of Anápolis – where I offered my services – insisted that I should look for a smaller city in the vicinity of Anápolis in order to avoid problems with the medical category. Decil is my personal friend. We went to Abadiânia and its mayor offered great support for my settling there.

Besides this political intervention there was a recommendation on the part of the spirit Bezerra de Menezes through Chico Xavier, whom I admired very much. Chico received a message from this spirit advising me to found a house for the practice of charity in the small town of Abadiânia, located in a region full of magnetism.

Why was the name "Casa de Dom Inácio" chosen?

This name came up spontaneously. I have always considered Saint Ignatius a great benefactor. The first procedure carried out through my mediation in Abadiânia was childbirth and it was performed by the Entity of Saint Ignatius. He is always looking over the Casa, therefore I named

---

[20]Decil de Sá Abreu was a public prosecutor and retired as a public attorney. He was the mayor of Anápolis in 1979 and 1980.

this center for spiritual cures in Abadiânia "Casa de Dom Inácio" as a tribute to him. There are two Casa de Dom Inácio houses in the states of Espírito Santo and Rio Grande do Sul and even abroad, all of which have established some sort of reference to Casa de Dom Inácio located in Abadiânia. I have a farm called Dom Inácio and there is a room in my house called Sala Dom Inácio ("Saint Ignatius Room") which is where I welcome people who seek me.

Have you ever considered leaving Abadiânia?

Yes. I once complained to Chico Xavier that I was deeply annoyed because I was being persecuted and that I intended to leave Abadiânia. He wrote me a note, which I still keep with great affection, which said: "João, your mission lies in Abadiânia."

Do you offer services in other cities and even in other countries?

Yes, as often as possible.

In which countries other than Brazil have you performed your mediumistic procedures?

As far as I remember I have been to the United States, Portugal, Spain, Greece, Germany, Bolivia, Peru, Paraguay, Argentina, and New Zealand.

Is it true that the Peruvian medical category tried to prevent you from performing cures?

Yes, but everything was sorted out in the end.[21]

---

[21] The medium João traveled to Peru several times, always tending to thousands of people – especially in poorer areas –, which resulted in hundreds of spiritual cures. There was an intense reaction on the part of the medical category concerning such cures and the medium was actually threatened with imprisonment. Several doctors also benefited from spiritual healing.

Even though the medium João acted as a mere instrument of Entities he was honored by the then president of Peru, who was himself treated of atrophy in his hand.

In one of João's trips to the region of Puno, more than 1,000 km from Lima, High Court Judge Liberato Póvoa from Tocantins state was a member of the medium's entourage and presents thrilling details in his book *João de Deus* – Fenômeno de Abadiânia.

You have worked in the Army. What was this experience like?

I was unemployed in Brasília when a person who had been healed by the Entities – using me as an apparatus – recommended me as a tailor in order to make uniforms. It was a calm period which brings me good memories.[22]

If you felt protected and happy, why did you leave the job at the Army?

As a shoemaker I worked for military officers and people they recommended, but I felt that my mission was to serve everybody.

4. Mediumship

When did your mediumship begin?
When I was 9 years old and lived in Itapaci.

What was this first manifestation of mediumship like?

I had been on my way from Itapaci to a village a few kilometers away with my mother when I told her there would be a violent storm and many houses would be destroyed. The sky was clear and my mother told me off for speaking such nonsense. But when we arrived at the village of Ponte Nova, we saw that a violent storm had in fact occurred and dozen of houses were destroyed.

What was the first cure by visible surgery performed through you?

The first cure by visible surgery happened in Campo Grande, Mato Grosso State. I was 16 years old at the time. The received Entity was King Solomon.[23]

---

[22] The medium João had been a victim of many injustices and persecutions because of his healing services. He went to work in the Army at the time of the military government. Somehow he was protected from persecutions. He remained a shoemaker at the Army for nine years.

[23] João was in the city of Campo Grande, the capital of the state of Mato Grosso do Sul, and found himself unemployed and undergoing financial difficulties. One day, when walking past a bridge, he decided to take a dip and, as he neared the water, he saw a beautiful woman with whom he talked all day. On the following day he returned to the place with the wish of seeing the woman. However, on the spot where she had stood he saw flashes of light and heard her voice telling him to look for Cristo Redentor Spiritist center. Under the guidance of the voice he went to the center, where he was expected. Unconsciously he performed several surgeries. When he regained consciousness he concluded he had fainted of hunger.

Are you aware of what happens when you are incorporated?

I do not see anything and I am not aware of anything. I feel as if I am sleeping. I am only an instrument of the Entities. It would actually be interesting to be able to see what goes on, but this is not possible.

How many Entities incorporate in you?

Several, I am not concerned about the exact number. Many send energy without incorporation.

Why does not the majority of Entities identify themselves?

Names are not important.

For what reason do you receive several spirits in the practice of healing, whereas other mediums receive only one spirit, such as Zé Arigó, who only received Dr. Fritz?

It simply happens that way, it is part of my mission.

You are not a Spiritist. What is your religion?

I am a Catholic, but religion is not important, we are all children of God. All religions must be respected.

Is not spiritual healing performed by your mediation typical of Spiritism?

My mission has nothing to do with religion. I met Chico Xavier and I have deep admiration for his work and for Spiritism, just as I respect Protestants. Mediumship does not depend on religion. Religion is a human creation but mediumship is not. Christ preached about love and charity without any tendency to any religious sect whatsoever.

How does incorporation occur?

Whenever I feel "radiation", it takes one or two seconds for incorporation to begin.

How can "radiation" be defined for non-experts?

"Radiation" is a "message", a kind of "note" or "sign". When I feel intense spiritual peace and a feeling of indestructible happiness, this is the "sign" that incorporation will follow.

When does de-incorporation occur, in the Entity room or when you retire to the resting room?

In the Entity room. I leave it a little dizzy from radiation and need some rest in order to get my strength back.

Besides incorporation based on free will, does involuntary incorporation exist?

It happens.

It is said that when you were first shown the recording of a surgery in which you were incorporated, you did not feel well. Is it true?

Yes, it is. As I said before, I feel as if I am asleep when I am incorporated. I was aware that I performed surgeries but I did not have any accurate knowledge of what happened. When I saw the tape with the entire surgical proceedings the shock was indeed great.

Why do some people obtain cures and others do not?

Merit.

Is it possible for someone to obtain a spiritual cure even without believing, without having faith?

Yes, but if someone has sought help this is already an indication of faith.

Is it possible to interview the medium João-in-Entity, in other words, to interview the Entity directly?

Yes.

Is it possible for a medium to give an answer provided by the Entity without being aware of it?

Yes, it happens all the time.

Is it a tiring routine to tend to people every Wednesdays, Thursdays, and Fridays and even on other weekdays outside Casa de Dom Inácio?

I try to fulfill my mission in the best way possible. Everybody should have a day in the week to rest. The majority rests on Sundays. My Sunday is on Tuesday. I have already grown accustomed to it, so it is really not a problem.

Are you able to heal someone without being incorporated?

No, as I said, I do not heal anyone, it is God who heals. I am only an instrument of the Entities. I am an ordinary person when I am not incorporated.

Are you capable of influencing spirits to heal a given person?

No. As an ordinary person I can only pray and wish for someone's well-being, but it is beyond my ability to interfere in any way so that this person is healed. When incorporated I serve as an instrument for good spirits to perform healing, if that is the case.

Have you ever had disappointments because of performed cures?

Yes, many times. When a person is healed and then goes back to a careless life I am sad.

I was also quite anguished, on the verge of tears, when a judge told me that I was the accused on a criminal lawsuit, not the spirit.[24]

Have people close to you, whose names need not be mentioned, tried to receive material benefits through your mediumship?

Yes, all the time.

What is your relationship with the medical category?

I can honestly say that it is the best relationship possible. I have many friends who are doctors. As far as spiritual healing is concerned, I respect those who do not believe in them.

Do you have notions of medicine or of human anatomy?

No, I have no knowledge of either. As I said, I am only an instrument of good spirits.

What kind of illnesses are cured at Casa de Dom Inácio?

No physical or psychic illness is beyond the possibility of cure. What is in fact not possible through modern scientific knowledge is possible through the knowledge of good spirits.

---

[24] During one of several cross-examinations the medium João, when questioned by the magistrate on his conduct of illegal practice of medicine, answered that he knew nothing of what occurred when incorporated, for he saw nothing and was not aware of what went on. The judge warned him in a strict manner that it was he, João Teixeira de Faria, who was being criminally sued, not the spirit incorporated by him.

When there is no concentration on the part of assistant mediums, do you tire more?

Yes, because a weak current demands more energy on my part.

From your first spiritual manifestation at the age of 9 until the present interview, has there been any interruption of service?

Yes, only when I was extremely ill. When I am ill but still in conditions to attend, I receive those who come looking for me.

Do people mix up the medium Jõao and the Entity?

Yes, all the time. I only try to listen to people.

If your mediumship is a mission, when will it be complete?

Only God knows. I accept this mission and I try to fulfill it as best as I can.

Do you know how long you will continue serving as an instrument for spiritual healing?

As long as I fulfill my mission with love and dedication. I will no longer be an instrument of healing on the day that I charge for an appointment.

How does one know if a person will or will not be healed?

Only the Entities know this because they are the ones who perform healing.

5. Prescribed medication

An infusion of plants was prescribed in the past, but now it has been replaced by Passiflora.[25] What is the reason for this change?

The effects are the same because both plants and Passiflora capsules are energized by good spirits. The infusion of plants is more difficult to prepare and there were many problems with inspection. Passiflora is prepared and wrapped by a pharmacist in strict accordance with legal norms.

---

[25] Passiflora is passion fruit powder (ground leaves and flowers).

From a medical perspective Passiflora is only a tranquillizer and it is the only prescribed medicine. How does it heal?

The medication is energized by the Entities in a specific way for each person. Even though everybody apparently receives the same medication there are differences in spiritual terms.

Appointments and surgeries are not charged. Why is Passiflora sold?

On the day that I charge for an appointment or a surgery I will lose my mediumship. I freely offer what I was freely given. As for Passiflora, which is the only prescribed medicine, it is produced in a laboratory with a pharmacist in charge, so the production involves costs. Profit obtained from the sale of Passiflora helps to maintain Casa de Dom Inácio. The Entity knows when a person cannot afford the medication and nothing is charged. If one day the Entities decide that no one should be charged, then the medication will be freely given to all.[26]

6. Other information

At Casa de Dom Inácio all people are regarded as equal, one is not more important than the other, their social status matters little. Nevertheless, have you ever been particularly touched by any situation?

Yes, several times. When someone is thankful and tells me he/she is healed, I am extremely satisfied.

Approximately how many people have been attended and how many cures have been performed with you as an apparatus?

I do not know. I believe that millions of people have been treated in more than forty years of mediumship. I am not aware of how many have reached spiritual healing.

You have treated several important people, such as politicians, businessmen, authorities, and celebrities. Among those who were healed in Abadiânia is the famous American actress Shirley MacLaine. Is this true?

Personally – as João Teixeira – I do not remember her, but it is true that she was attended and healed by the Entities at Casa de Dom Inácio.[27]

---

[26] For more information on Passiflora see Chapter V, n. 13.

[27] It is said that Shirley MacLaine was operated on by the medium João Teixeira when incorporated and that she left the service room screaming with happiness, saying that she felt no more pains and that she was cured. This was the subject of a report by the magazine Revista Manchete on March 16 and March 30, 1991 (PÓVOA, Liberato. In: *João de Deus* – Fenômeno de Abadiânia, p. 74).

It is said that an American opera singer who had lost her voice[28] was cured at Casa de Dom Inácio. What was this case like?

The cure was as normal as with hundreds of victims of infirmities. The interesting thing was that, after being cured, the singer returned to Abadiânia and sang in a performance for those present. She said that she was keeping her promise of singing in Abadiânia before returning to her artistic performances in New York.

Describe the problem at Mondongo Farm.

In an isolated ranch within the farm in the town of Pirenópolis lived eight farm workers who were victims of physical manifestations of low vibration spirits. At a request I went to the farm where prayers were performed at first. After some time, the suffering spirits were pacified and everything went back to normal.[29]

Was there a special case regarding the madness of the son of an influential American politician?

Yes, there was. A certain politician – who later became my friend – had a son with serious obsession problems. The Entities used me as a mediumistic channel and performed several disobsession sessions. As a result, the young man began to have an almost normal conduct.[30]

---

[28] Witnesses to this story revealed that the singer had throat cancer.

[29] Mondongo Farm is located in the town of Pirenópolis, more than 50 km from Abadiânia. This episode happened in 1990. Physical manifestations included a series of aggressions on the farm workers: beatings, slaps, throwing of stones and dirt, moving objects, appearance of strange objects etc. The entire event was registered by a journalist of Diário da Manhã – Goiânia (idem, ibidem, p. 67).

[30] This story involved a highly influential individual, both politically and economically, from Miami (USA), whose son had serious problems of obsession which may even have been regarded as possession (a spiritual illness which causes a person to be completely overpowered by the obsessing spirit and to act like a furious lunatic). The situation went to such extremes that the young man was actually locked up. After being submitted to mediumistic treatment his condition improved considerably. He became peaceful and friendly and started to accompany his father in his social and commercial activities. The medium João did not accept any kind of reward because he knew that it had been God and not he who had promoted healing. The young man's father tried to convince the medium João to move to Miami and remain close to his son, and in return he would pay for the medium's expenses. However João did not accept the offer because he knew that his mission involved tending to the greatest number of people possible.

It is remarked that even women who had been unable to get pregnant, despite intense medical treatment, were finally able to have children after spiritual treatment at Casa de Dom Inácio. Is this true?

Yes, it is. I know of several real stories because parents invited me to be godfather to their children. I have godchildren all the way from Roraima to Rio Grande do Sul. I pray for all my godchildren to be happy.

How many honors (citizenship, honor award, companion, friend of the city etc.) have been granted to you in acknowledgement of your work?

I have been granted more than 100 honors, which were given by mayors, city halls, and several organizations. Since it is not possible to pay direct tribute to spirits these are paid to me. On the other hand, since it is not possible to sue criminally good spirits that perform healing, I am the one who is sued.

Have you ever performed surgery on yourself?

No, I was operated on by the Entities through my apparatus.[31] Many consider this as "self-surgery" but I was never aware of what I was doing.

Is there a constant search for information by the press on Casa de Dom Inácio?

Yes, I believe this happens more with the foreign press than with the Brazilian press.

Have you ever been researched by scientists?

Yes, especially by foreigners. I do not have further details at hand but I know of studies that have been carried out by scientists. Whenever such a request is made it is attended to.[32]

---

[31] For more information on the subject see Chapter V, n. 18.

[32] The medium João has already served as a research object for American, German, Italian, Canadian, English, and French scientists. Among the studies in the field of Parapsychology is the research carried out by Paul Louis Laussac, director of the *Advanced Science Research and Development Corporation* in Georgia and head of research of the *Psychotronic Corporation of Advanced Nature Concepts* in Los Angeles, California (USA). His study was revealed to the public on the TV program *Terceira Visão* (Third Vision) broadcasted by Rede Bandeirante de Televisão. João was also part of a research by German Parapsychologist Klaus Schubert (University of Freiburg – Germany) and by American scientists Lloyd Youngblood (*American Society of Dowsers*), William J. Rudge, and Bill Cooks (*Innerspace Explorations S/E Inc.*). PÓVOA, Liberato. In: *João de Deus* – Fenômeno de Abadiânia, p. 68/75).

The outstanding number of foreigners who attend Casa de Dom Inácio (Americans, Canadians, English, Portuguese, Spanish, Irish, French, Italians, Germans, Swiss, Greek, Australians, and people from other countries) is impressive. How does this occur and how is the communication barrier overcome?

There are guides who organize journeys in various countries. Casa de Dom Inácio also has interpreters who help to establish communication.[33]

Brazil has been a frequent stage for unexplainable phenomena related to spiritual healing. Are there any reasons for this?

What I can say is that several people regarded by science as paranormals come forward in Brazil.

What is your opinion of Chico Xavier, Zé Arigó, and Edson Queiroz?

Chico Xavier is beyond any kind of comment, whereas other mediums, healers or not, have a mission to fulfill.

Is it possible for "low vibration spirits" to influence mediumistic manifestations negatively? Does this happen at Casa de Dom Inácio?

No. As a medium I pray and place my apparatus at the service of good spirits. The "current" formed by assistant mediums and the "energy" offered by the Casa's protecting spirits prevent any interference from spirits that do not desire people's well-being.[34]

When you disincarnate will Casa de Dom Inácio close its doors or will there be a substitute who will act as an apparatus in order to receive spirits and continue work on spiritual healing?

All I can say is that Casa de Dom Inácio will continue to exist regardless of myself.

---

[33] See Chapter III, n. 11.
[34] See Chapter V, n. 4.

Chapter III

Casa de Dom Inácio

Visitors who first arrive at Casa de Dom Inácio wish to know what this place is like and how it works. Answers were provided by interviews with the medium João, directors, collaborators, and regular visitors, as well as by the author's personal observations.

1. Abadiânia

Why was the town of Abadiânia chosen for the establishment of Casa de Dom Inácio?

It was the medium João's personal choice, whose reasons were explained in Chapter II, n. 3.

What useful information may be given regarding the town of Abadiânia?

- Location: Goiás State, between Brasília – capital of Brazil – and Goiânia – capital of Goiás; to the north are Corumbá de Goiás and Alexânia; to the south is Silvânia, and to the west are Anápolis and Pirenópolis;
- Population: approximately 13,000 inhabitants;
- Area: 1,046 km²;
- Climate: tropical savanna with a rainy season during the summer (October/April) and a dry season during the winter (May/September). Temperatures are normally very high;
- Electrical voltage: 220 volts;
- Altitude: varies from 800 m to 1,000 m above sea level;
- Soil: little erosion, highly acid clay texture which requires some correction for agricultural use;
- Vegetation: Cerrado landscape with fruit trees;
- Hydrography: das Antas, Capivari, and Corumbá rivers are the most important in the region;
- Origin of name: "Abadia" (in honor of the patron saint) and "Nia" (in honor of the founder Emericiana);
- Foundation: 1914, with annual sessions of simple prayers promoted by the town's first resident, Dona Emericiana.

Are the initial headquarters of Abadiânia still in use today?

There has indeed been a change of headquarters. Initially two communities were affectionately called Velha Abadiânia (Old Abadiânia) and Nova Abadiânia (New Abadiânia). As the years went by the latter became simply known as Abadiânia.

47

How far is Velha Abadiânia from present-day headquarters?

18 km.

How did Nova Abadiânia come to life?

The foundation of Brasília stirred in politicians of the period a desire to move headquarters to the vicinities of the BR-060 highway and therefore promote the town's progress. In addition, the town would stand at approximately the same distance from both Brasília and Goiânia.

How far is Abadiânia from Brasília, Anápolis, and Goiânia?

The distance between Brasília and Abadiânia will depend on the exact location of the capital that one takes as a reference point. It is common to use the airport, the bus station, or even the Esplanada dos Ministérios (Esplanade of Ministries) as reference, so the distance to Abadiânia will obviously be altered. If one takes as reference the Federal District's Highway Police Post (exit to Goiânia) the distance between Brasília and Abadiânia will be around 95 km.

The distance from Abadiânia to Anápolis and from Abadiânia to Goiânia will also be different depending on reference points. There are approximately 35 km between Abadiânia and Anápolis' first intersection and about 85 km between Abadiânia and the intersection at Goiânia's main entrance point (Anhangüera Avenue). Obviously the distance will increase if the reference point is the city center.

How many hotels and inns ("pousadas") are there in Abadiânia?

Approximately thirty.

How many beds are there in total?

Approximately 1,500 beds.

If someone wishes to stay in a more sophisticated hotel in Abadiânia, is it possible?

No, the nearest options are located in Anápolis, Goiânia, and Brasília.

Do regular buses from Goiânia to Brasília and from Brasília to Goiânia stop in Abadiânia?

Yes, there are buses many times every day.

How many taxis are there in Abadiânia?

More than thirty running licensed taxis.

Are there rentable houses in Abadiânia?

Yes, there are fully furnished houses which are rented only for a few months. However, such commercial activity is not linked with Casa de Dom Inácio.

Does the medium João live in Abadiânia?

No. Even though he has an apartment at Casa de Dom Inácio and a farm in town he actually lives in Anápolis, a city of over 300,000 people. One may say that he has a double residence. His residence at Casa de Dom Inácio is useful when he needs to spend the night in Abadiânia.

2. Casa de Dom Inácio – what is it like?

How can Casa de Dom Inácio be defined?

Casa de Dom Inácio is a place where spiritual healing is performed. It is a house of prayers, charity, and love. Many call it a spiritual hospital. It is not a Spiritist center nor a church but a place where worshippers of different religions meet. Therefore, it would not be wrong to call it an ecumenical temple.

The following objective is part of its statute: "To perform spiritual, moral, and material charity, by all means within its reach, without distinction of sex, race, religious creed, or political and philosophical convictions, and without any expectations of retribution."

What is the reason for the name "Casa de Dom Inácio"?

The name was personally chosen by the medium João.

What is Casa de Dom Inácio from a legal perspective?

Casa de Dom Inácio is a non-profit juridical person of private right and of an associative-beneficent nature. It possesses a Statute and an Internal Regiment which are duly registered in accordance with legal norms. The Casa has an elected board of directors led by its president, the medium João.

What was Casa de Dom Inácio like at the beginning?

After having performed his services in several places throughout Brazil the medium João started doing so regularly and permanently in Abadiânia. There were many setbacks in the beginning. Casa de Dom Inácio initially functioned in many different houses on a temporary basis until the present location – a farm – was acquired. Proceedings were simple at the beginning but eventually progressed thanks to resources provided by the medium João and by donations and collaborations from regular visitors.

Does religious practice recommend sophisticated temples?

That depends on the religion. Places of worship of different religions are necessary, but whether they should be sophisticated or not depends on each religious segment.

It is a known fact that Spiritism has simple temples, whereas other religions prefer sumptuous temples.

Is Casa de Dom Inácio a simple or a sumptuous place?

Simplicity prevails at Casa de Dom Inácio, but this does not mean that it is a Spiritist center.[35] Buildings are modest, though clean and well-kept.

What is the Casa's furniture like?

The furniture is also quite simple, some items are even rustic.

Is the Casa open every evening?

Yes.

Is there any connection between the local inns and Casa de Dom Inácio?

None whatsoever. Whereas inns have commercial aims, the Casa possesses spiritual ones. Local inns are organized in an association[36] which is not linked in any way with Casa de Dom Inácio.

Do inn owners help the Casa in any way?

Several owners are voluntary workers in proceedings at the Casa due to spiritual cures they previously received.

---

[35] There are various images and portraits of saints at Casa de Dom Inácio. Spiritists and Protestants do not worship images or saints.

[36] Associação das Pousadas e Hotéis de Abadiânia (APHA) (Association of Inns and Hotels of Abadiânia).

Does Casa de Dom Inácio have its own website, which allows those interested to obtain more information?

No. The board of directors understands that the establishment should not produce any kind of publicity.

However, there are websites of guides and inns as well as a website called *Amigos da Casa de Dom Inácio* (Friends of Casa de Dom Inácio), produced by people who benefited from spiritual healing.

Does the Casa have an electronic mail address?

No.

Are services at the Casa interrupted whenever the medium João travels abroad?

No, it continues functioning normally with lectures, prayers, distribution of fluidified water etc. The only procedure that does not occur is the service of the medium João-in-Entity.

Whenever the medium João travels abroad notices regarding his absence are given in advance. When attendance occurs in other locations outside Abadiânia it is performed from Saturdays to Tuesdays.

3. Physical space

What is the physical area of Casa de Dom Inácio like?

Casa de Dom Inácio covers a total area of more than 12,000 m² and features a parking lot, a rest area, a mediumistic area, an administrative area, a snack bar, a bookshop, a Passiflora processing and wrapping factory, a crystal bath room, public toilets, public telephones, a taxi stop, and the medium João's apartment.

How are the buildings distributed throughout Casa de Dom Inácio's total area?

The sketches presented at the end of this chapter offer a general idea of the distribution of the area. Figure 1 (p. 84) is a panoramic plant of the total area and Figure 2 (p. 85) reveals the entire division of the mediumistic area.

Does the Casa offer toilets for the public?

Yes, several, both for men and women, which include facilities for people with locomotion difficulties.

Are there public telephones?

Yes.

Is attendance disturbed when it rains?

Problems exist for those arriving at the Casa but not for those who are already within its limits. Therefore, queue services are attended normally.

Does the rain disturb the movement of those outside the covered area?

The terrain of the Casa is fairly plain and drained. Setbacks are natural and typical of any place during rain.

4. Parking lot

What is the parking lot like?

As the expression itself indicates, it is the physical space where visitors of the Casa can park their vehicles, both private vehicles and buses and taxis from other locations.

Is the parking lot large enough for private vehicles, taxis, and buses which take visitors to the Casa?

Normally yes. There is a large area in front of the Casa which, even though it does not belong to it, is lent for parking whenever necessary.

There is a taxi stop at the Casa's front yard. Do the taxis belong to the establishment?

No, the taxi stop is there so vehicles are able to attend visitors in an orderly way. They remain outside the Casa's complex and only a few are authorized to remain within the internal parking area. All taxis are of private property and licensed by the city hall. The Casa has nothing to do with this activity.

5. Rest area

What is the rest area?

It is a physical space which covers the gardens, the viewpoint, and the verandas.

What are the gardens like?

They may be referred to as green areas with grassy patches, typical Cerrado trees, fruit trees, and flowers. There are also several cement walks and rustic benches for people to rest on.

What types of fruit trees are grown at Casa de Dom Inácio?
Mango trees, cashew trees, guava trees etc.

What happens during fruit season?
There is no concern over the fruits, they ripen and are picked by visitors.

Is the rest area used by those who took part in morning procedures and wait for afternoon procedures?
Yes. Soup is served for free at the Casa and to many people this soup acts as lunch. Those who wish to rest go to the inns (this happens with participants of journey groups) but several people remain resting at the Casa.

Is there enough space for those who await afternoon procedures?
Yes. Apart from the gardens with fruit trees which offer shade and benches for more than 200 people, the viewpoint and the verandas also provide seats.

What is the viewpoint?
The viewpoint is a kind of veranda[37] with a beautiful view of the entire valley surrounding Casa de Dom Inácio. It is a calm place and a popular area among visitors.

How many seated people fit in the viewpoint?
Approximately fifty people.

How many verandas are there at the Casa?
Several, many of which have benches or walls that serve as seats.

6. Mediumistic area

What is the mediumistic area?
It is the most important part of Casa de Dom Inácio because it is the place where spiritual healing is performed.

How is the mediumistic area divided?
It comprises an assembly hall; assistant mediums' room; Entity rooms; a prayer room; a ward (or recovery room); a rest room; a video

---

[37] Verandas: covered and open areas (without walls); yard; balcony; terrace.

and sound room; a room of wheelchairs, prosthesis, and crutches; a diploma room; a mail room; storage areas; verandas and private toilets.

How many seats are there in the assembly hall?

Approximately 200 seats.

Why is there a stage-like platform in the assembly hall where queues are formed?

The platform is used by those who make announcements to the public on procedures and by those who conduct the opening talk and therefore need to be visible to all those present.

How many Entity rooms are there?

Three rooms, two of which are occupied by assistant mediums (sons and daughters of the Casa) and a third which, at the start of works, is occupied by people who will be submitted to group surgeries. After the people in such group surgeries leave the room, chairs are then occupied by people invited by the Entity to "sit in the current" while it proceeds to individual services. The three rooms are interconnected and constitute a single space which totals more than 280 chairs occupied by mediums. The latter form an energizing current of support for the works under way.

The first room, right beyond the assembly hall, is occupied by mediums in charge of preparatory "cleansing". Such cleansing removes all negative energy so that a person receives a more thorough and effective treatment by the Entity.

How many people can be seated in the Entity rooms?

The queues' entrance room, occupied by assistant mediums: 100.

The Entity's main room, occupied by assistant mediums: 100.

The room for guests in current work: 80.

In addition to fixed chairs, extra ones are placed whenever necessary.

Is there a ward at the Casa?

There is a large room with twelve beds. It is not an actual ward but a recovery room, where people who are individually submitted to spiritual healing remain until they recover their strength and go home, which takes from 1 to 2 hours.

What is the prayer room like?

At the start of work this room is occupied by people who will be submitted to group surgeries. There are chairs and fixed stretchers for anyone who needs them. When all the chairs are occupied – and this often happens – people are settled in one of the assistant mediums' room. Those who do not speak Portuguese are seated apart from Brazilians in order to make the interpreter's job easier.

Several mediums remain in the room after group surgeries are concluded and offer prayers for those who were attended by the Entity.

How many chairs and stretchers are there in the prayer room?

Sixty chairs and five stretchers.

What are the lighting facilities in the mediumistic area?

In addition to artificial lighting (electrical lamps) and windows, the mediumistic area has three large skylights[38], two indoors and the other in the assembly hall. Sunlight is necessary due to the energy radiated from it.

Which images are displayed in this area?

Images of Jesus Christ, Saint Ignatius of Loyola, Our Lady of Fatima, Saint Teresa, and Our Lady Aparecida, among others.

Which portraits (pictures and photographs) are displayed on the walls?

There are several, which include: Jesus Christ, Saint Ignatius of Loyola, King Solomon, Osvaldo Cruz, Chico Xavier, Our Lady of Fatima, Pope John Paul II, Bezerra de Menezes, Mother Teresa of Calcutta, Eurípedes Barsanulfo, Augusto de Almeida, and João de Deus.

Are there other frames on the walls?

Yes, there are several messages, poems, sonnets, thoughts, and prayers in frames all over the walls in the mediumistic area.

---

[38] Skylight: elevation on the roof with glass windows on the sides which allow the sunlight into the room.

Are the paintings and images acquired by the Casa administration?

No, they are all donations of Casa visitors.

What is the rest room used for?

It acts as a kind of office and consultation room for the medium João in which Casa staff members are welcomed to discuss administrative affairs and people in general discuss private affairs. The medium João rarely stops for lunch, he has only a light snack and remains resting in order to recover his energies spent in morning procedures.

Is there a miracle room?

It is not correct to use the word "miracle". What can be found is a physical space in which wheelchairs, orthopedic devices of various kinds, and crutches are left by people benefited by spiritual healing.

7. Administrative area and staff

In what consists the administrative area?

It is a place which offers support for mediumistic works and comprises a management office, a general office, an information desk, a storage room, a kitchen, a dining room for staff, a public dining room, and toilets.

Who is responsible for carrying out daily administrative activities which are necessary for the proper functioning of the Casa?

The Casa has several members of staff in charge of different tasks as well as volunteers who work for free.

How many members of staff are there at Casa de Dom Inácio?

Over twenty registered workers with work cards signed by the employer.

What jobs do staff workers perform?

Attendance on visitors, cleaning, food preparation, maintenance, and general preservation of the Casa. The main member of staff is the administrator, a kind of general manager who is responsible for the entire administrative setting. The Casa also has cooks, an administrative secretary (as well as the secretary from the board of directors), office assistants, attendants, telephone operators, a drugstore assistant, a sound operator, a storekeeper, and janitors.

How are members of staff selected?

Whenever posts are vacant résumés are analyzed and candidates are interviewed. Those who meet the requirements are thus chosen by the Casa administrator.

If the Casa staff work during the break between morning and afternoon works, at what time do they have lunch?

During break between morning and afternoon procedures, after soup is served, those who wish to take part in afternoon works have several options of things to do, so staff members have lunch in shifts.

Attendance to the public takes place three days a week (Wednesdays, Thursdays, and Fridays). Is the Casa closed on the other weekdays (Saturdays, Sundays, Mondays, and Tuesdays) and are staff members dismissed?

No, administrative work continues despite the small public. The labor right of weekly rest is duly respected via a rota system. Obviously there is much more work to be done on the three days of attendance, but there are still activities on non-attendance days. The administrative office works from Mondays to Fridays, from 7 am to 6 pm.

Who are the volunteers, in other words, the people who provide administrative and mediumistic services without receiving payment?

The word "volunteer" says it all. The number of volunteers is indeed great and includes people from other countries who leave on holiday in order to work at Casa de Dom Inácio. The majority of volunteers offer their services as a kind of retribution for obtained cures.

Several people wear identification badges with their names and job posts on them. Are they all staff members of the Casa?

Not only staff members wear such badges, but many volunteers and guides as well. The aim is to make the identification of those who assist in procedures more accessible to the general public.

8. Snack bar

What is the snack bar like?

It is similar to so many others. It does not have seats in the indoor area, only walls which serve as seats outside.

What is sold at the snack bar?

Various juices, coconut water, coffee, milk, sweets, chocolates, pastries, ice-cream, mineral water, cold drinks, among other products typical of snack bars.

What are the snack bar's working hours?

It is open from Wednesdays to Fridays, from 6 am to 6 pm like any normal commercial establishment. It is licensed as a small business.

Are people forbidden to take their own snack to the Casa because of the snack bar?

Not at all, the snack bar attends people who need some sort of quick snack without having to leave the Casa. Therefore, people may take snacks if they want to.

During the intervals between morning and afternoon works it is common to find whole families having snacks out on the green areas or by the parked vehicles.

9. Bookshop

What is the bookshop like?

It is a small shop, in fact it resembles more a bazaar than a bookshop.

What is sold at the bookshop?

Books, T-shirts, crystals, rosaries, jewellery, fluidified water, and various souvenirs.

What are the bookshop's working hours?

They are similar to those of the snack bar: it is open to the public from 6 am to 6 pm (from 7 am to 12 pm on weekends). It is a small business which follows all legal requirements and its staff members are duly registered.

Is fluidified water sold there?

Yes, fluidified water is sold at the bookshop in amounts that visitors wish to take home. Normal mineral water is sold at the snack bar. Fluidified water is freely offered by the Casa for those who wish to drink it there.

It is not uncommon for the Entity to prescribe fluidified water for all the assistant mediums present. When that happens fluidified mineral water is freely distributed in transportable containers.

Why is fluidified water sold?

It must be said that this mineral water is properly bottled and that the price charged for it is not superior to that of any commercial establishment. There is no extra charge for fluidification.

10. Regular visitors

Who attends Casa de Dom Inácio?

People from all parts of Brazil and from many countries.

Is some form of entrance control adopted within the establishment?

No, entrance is free of charge even for cars or buses. Anyone wishing to enter, observe, and take part in procedures may do so.

Is a person who attends Casa de Dom Inácio for the first time likely to feel a little lost?

If a person is part of an excursion, which is often the case, then he/she will follow the group guide who provides all the necessary information. There are several members of staff who provide assistance to those who go to the Casa on their own. There is also an information desk at the Casa office where a member of staff attends the general public. In addition any visitor will have the greatest pleasure in providing the necessary information. Interpreters are available for those who do not speak Portuguese.

Staff members, guides, and volunteers who assist in procedures are identified by badges.

Do children attend the Casa?

Yes, but they are duly accompanied by parents or guardians, just as elderly people who have difficulties in locomotion or other problems are accompanied by relatives or friends.

Children are usually restless. How is noise produced by children dealt with at the Casa?

This has not been a problem at the Casa.

Do doctors attend the Casa?

Yes, several.

In addition to doctors, do other people with high cultural status attend the Casa?

Yes, regular visitors include court judges, public prosecutors, police chiefs, lawyers, engineers, individuals with various university degrees, military officers etc.

Do doctors, artists, journalists, authorities, and celebrities receive special treatment?

No, every person who seeks the Casa receives equal treatment, without discrimination of color, sex, age, cultural background, religion, social status, nationality etc.

Are there more male or female visitors?

It is not important and escapes one's notice. It appears to be equal in proportion.

Is there any recorded data regarding age, level of formal education, marital status, religion etc.?

No, the Casa has no concerns regarding such records.

Some people carry out research for scientific or academic purposes and go about gathering information. The following table presents data collected by a psychologist[39] during the field work for her post-graduate thesis:

---

[39] SAVARIS, Alfredina Arlete. *Curas Paranormais Realizadas por João Teixeira de Faria*, p. 84/86.

a) Age
   under 18....................13,60%
   18 to 25....................21,60%
   26 to 35....................27,00%
   36 to 45....................23,00%
   above 46...................14,80%

b) Level of formal education
   primary education......51,80%
   secondary education..35,20%
   higher education........13,00%

c) Marital Status
   single..........................27,00%
   married.....................48,60%
   divorced....................10,80%
   widowed..................13,60%

d) Religion
   Catholic......................62,00%
   Spiritist......................27,20%
   others..........................09,60%
   non-worshippers.........01,20%

e) Voluntary visit to the Casa?
   yes.............................78,80%
   no..............................21,20%

f) Presence of companion?
   yes..............................47,00%
   no...............................53,00%

g) Reason for seeking Casa de
   Dom Inácio
   health treatment........75,60%
   curiosity....................04,00%
   prayer........................18,80%
   other reasons.............01,60%

h) Attendance at the Casa
   less than 1 year...........60,20%
   1 to 3 years.................18,60%
   4 to 6 years.................18,20%
   above 7 years..............03,00%

Does the majority of people who seek Casa de Dom Inácio suffer from some form of handicap or physical illness?

Many are indeed physically handicapped and require the use of wheelchairs, crutches, walking sticks, or reveal some other form of visible physical problem. However the majority has no apparent physical problem. Instead they suffer from existential troubles and seek only a meaning for life.

If a person is absent from the Casa for some time and one day returns with a different health problem, what happens?

The Entity recognizes this person no matter how much time has passed since the previous attendance. A new procedure is performed normally.

Are individuals who attend morning works the same as those attending afternoon works?

Not all of them. There is no control relating to regular visits at the Casa. It all depends on whether a person wishes to participate or not. In countless situations the Entity asks a person to return in the afternoon or on the next day.

Those who travel in groups either from other states in Brazil or from other countries are able to make the most not only of both periods in one day but of both periods during several days.

Is the Casa open to the public during non-attendance hours?

The Casa gates remain open every day from 7 am to 9 pm.

It is common for people in tours – tours which remain several days in Abadiânia - to visit the Casa outside normal opening hours for meditation both at the viewpoint and in the assembly hall.

Does the number of visitors suffer variations due to socioeconomic problems?

Yes. Even though treatment does not offer any expenses, trip and accommodation costs for those who live a long way from Abadiânia – especially for foreign visitors – are high. Therefore, the possibility of affording such expenses depends on an individual's financial situation at a given moment, so socioeconomic hardships do affect the number of visitors who seek Casa de Dom Inácio. This is true both for Brazilians and for foreigners.

It is a known fact that countless people who would like to travel to Abadiânia are not in a condition to afford travel expenses, despite the free treatment provided at the Casa. Such difficulties are partly solved when a tour guide or a friend takes a person's photograph or a personal object (mostly items of clothing) and returns with the prescribed medication.

Are regular visitors always the same?

No. Usually people who receive spiritual healing do not return to the Casa anymore after a given period. Countless others have followed the medium João for decades. Several volunteers in administrative posts and assistant mediums have participated sporadically in procedures for over 25 years. It is common to meet people who have been attending the Casa for 5, 10, 15, and 20 years.

Can a person who does not return to the Casa be considered ungrateful after having benefited from healing?

No, people are free to return if and when they please. As the Casa is not a temple of a specific religion, a person who benefited from spiritual healing may attend – and this is a common occurrence – the temple of his/her own religion. The Entity often says that a person is cured and that he/she may return to the Casa at leisure if he/she wishes. Many actually return in order to offer thanks, to reveal exam results, to show evidence of their cures, to accompany others in search of treatment, or to act as volunteers.

Is it common for people to remain a long time in Abadiânia in order to attend the Casa?

Yes, but this is not necessary. The Entity states when a given person should return so he/she may carry out day-to-day activities normally.

11. Foreigners

A considerable number of foreigners who have difficulties in understanding Portuguese seek Casa de Dom Inácio. How is communication established?

There are several members of staff who speak enough English to establish communication. They act as interpreters whenever necessary. In addition, several guides and a few volunteers speak English, so communication problems are solved quite easily.

During attendance by the Entity each foreign visitor is accompanied by an interpreter who communicates with the Entity in Portuguese. Almost all foreign visitors who arrive at Casa de Dom Inácio speak English. Whenever there is a tour group whose members only speak the local language back in their country, there is always an English speaker in the group.

Nevertheless, the author has witnessed public announcements in Portuguese be repeated in English, French, and German due to the presence of tour groups from the United States, France, and Germany.

What leisure options are there for foreign visitors who remain more than one week in Abadiânia?

Many foreigners choose to visit Brasília, Goiânia, Pirenópolis, Cidade de Goiás, Caldas Novas etc, while others prefer to remain in Abadiânia.

Distances from Abadiânia to Brasília, Anápolis, and Goiânia were provided at the beginning of this chapter (Chapter III, n. 1). How far is Abadiânia from the following cities?

- Abadiânia to Pirenópolis: 52 Km;
- Abadiânia to Cidade de Goiás (via Goiânia): 270 km;
- Abadiânia to Cidade de Goiás (alternative route): 240 km;
- Abadiânia to Caldas Novas (via Bela Vista and Piracanjuba): 270 km;
- Abadiânia to Caldas Novas (via Bela Vista and Cristianópolis): 250 km;
- Abadiânia to Caldas Novas (via BR-153 highway and Piracanjuba): 280 km.

Do foreigners acquire houses in Abadiânia?

Yes, not only foreigners but Brazilians from other states as well. Some visitors choose to reside in Abadiânia and thus acquire houses in town, whereas other regular visitors acquire houses and lend them to friends, both Brazilians and foreigners.

12. Travel groups and guides

How are travel groups seeking Casa de Dom Inácio structured, be them from other Brazilian states or from other countries?

Regardless of the place of origin of travel groups, these are led by guides who are familiar with the daily routine of the Casa. Normally guides organize a "package" which includes land or air transportation and accommodation in one of Abadiânia's many inns.

It must be stated that Casa de Dom Inácio's administration has no relation with local inns and guides who organize such trips. From a commercial point of view there is no connection between inns and tour guides and Casa de Dom Inácio.

Many inn owners and guides are individuals who received cures at the Casa in the past and decided to embark on an activity which brings them psychological satisfaction.

How many guides who organize travel groups both in Brazil and abroad are known at the Casa?

Approximately fifty.

From which Brazilian states are the majority of travel groups?

Most travel groups are apparently from Rio Grande do Sul, Espírito Santo, Minas Gerais, Paraná, and Santa Catarina, because of indication given by Casa visitors.

From which countries are the majority of travel groups?

Most travel groups are apparently from the United States and Germany because of indication given by Casa visitors and effective organization of tours.

Is there some kind of appointment list for the arrival of travel groups at the Casa?

No, people may arrive at the Casa at any time and they will be attended to.

Do tour guides also help in procedures?

Yes, foreign tour guides help as interpreters and tour guides from other Brazilian locations help whenever necessary.

13. Infiltration

Are there ways of establishing contact with the Casa other than those previously described?

Yes, it is possible to enter the Casa motivated by reasons other than the search for spiritual healing.

Who are the individuals who enter the establishment with unorthodox intentions?

Journalists, doctors, police officers, and curious people in general.

How can one describe the visits of such individuals not seeking spiritual healing?

Both Brazilian and foreign journalists visit the Casa for professional reasons and many become regular visitors. Doctors who do not believe in spiritual healing go to the Casa with the single purpose of witnessing what happens there and, as a result, some also become regular visitors. Police officers arrive at the Casa with the aim of observing any irregularities and also end up as regular visitors and defenders of the medium João. Finally there are curious people.

Who are these "curious people" who attend the Casa?

Generally they are individuals who do not believe in spiritual cures or have doubts regarding their veracity.

What happens when such "curious people" arrive at the Casa?

The Casa is open for visiting by any person during non-working hours and even allows photography and filming. During working hours a person has to line up as usual and may observe at will.

Is infiltration - the act of entering a place with the purpose of establishing fraud - possible?

Yes, and it happens from time to time. In addition to entering the queue an individual may infiltrate among mediums and assistants. There are over 280 initially available chairs. Despite entrance control infiltration is possible.

Has infiltration of journalists - without interference or disturbance of procedures - happened in the past?

Yes.[40]

May attendance in Abadiânia be interrupted due to interference by journalists?

Yes, but it does not happen often because staff members are previously taught how to proceed in such cases.

Has this ever happened in places other than Abadiânia?

Yes, therefore the need for authorization and for guidance regarding photographers, cameramen, and interviewers and the way they should behave at the Casa.

In Germany there was one case of interruption of procedures because journalists had been attempting to interview people who were being attended to. There would not have been any problem if such interviews had been carried out before and/or after procedures, but they were basically carried out during procedures in a way that interfered with normal attendance. The Entity "rose" leaving around 500 people in queues, all of whom were eventually attended to the next day.

---

[40] For more information see Chapter IV, n. 5.

Therefore previous guidance is given in order to prevent setbacks which may disturb the efficacy of procedures.

Are procedures interrupted when research is involved?

No, because research studies receive authorization. Therefore, both the medium João-in-Entity and researchers are able to perform their work effectively.

Is the Casa not concerned a priori with possible infiltration on the part of journalists, police officers, and curious people in general?

No, for the Entity identifies the infiltrator and the reason for his/her visit. Whereas this is not extraordinary for Casa staff, it usually causes embarrassment for the exposed individual.

14. Service procedures

How can daily works in both periods be described?

Services follow standard procedure every Wednesdays, Thursdays, and Fridays, in the morning or in the afternoon. Initially a person receives the necessary guidance regarding attendance in the assembly hall and then enters queues known as first-time line, second-time line, 8 am and 2 pm lines, surgery line, and review line. Queues are formed after general announcements are given regarding attendance, prayers, and an initial talk by a Casa assistant. Afterwards people lined up in queues are called forward and individually attended to by the Entity.

Are standard procedures always the same?

Changes do occur from time to time in a natural evolution which continually aims to offer better services for those who seek the Casa. Those who are absent from the Casa for a long period do notice small changes. Nevertheless, procedures are essentially the same.

If one considers the great number of non-Portuguese speakers, does not attendance by the Entity drag due to the constant need of interpreting?

Prior to the start of procedures, in order to prevent long waits for services, two interpreters (members of staff, volunteers, or guides) listen to each foreign visitor individually and jots down on a piece of paper brief observations in Portuguese. People take this piece of paper with them and hand it over to an interpreter just before attendance by the Entity. The interpreter, having read beforehand what was recorded on the piece of paper, is able to speak to the Entity on behalf of the individual, and therefore waiting time is reduced.

Do procedures vary from one day to the next?

No, they are essentially the same, even though on some days more people arrive at the Casa and on others more spiritual surgeries are performed.

The author has often heard the Entity express satisfaction regarding the considerable number of "discharges" in a given day, but nothing relating to this matter is previously settled.

15. Assistant mediums, sons and daughters of the Casa

Who are the individuals sitting in the Entity rooms?

They are assistant mediums, sons and daughters of the Casa.

Who exactly are the sons and daughters of the Casa?

They are people who have created links with Casa de Dom Inácio, who have benefited from spiritual healing for themselves or for relatives, or who only desire to act as volunteers and aid in Casa procedures, especially as mediums.

How many sons and daughters of the Casa are there?

Approximately two thousands.

Who declares a person a son or a daughter of the Casa, the medium João or the Entity?

The Entity.

What are the criteria for declaring someone a son or a daughter of the Casa?

No one but the Entity knows.

What is the task performed by assistant mediums during attendance on the queues?

Mental concentration allows for the positive energizing of the environment in order to make it suitable for effective procedures.

How are assistants selected for daily work?

There is no actual selection. The sons and daughters of the Casa are volunteers who arrive spontaneously regardless of their religion. However there is a recommendation of appropriate times for improved efficacy in procedures.

How many volunteers assist in works at the Casa in a given day on average?

There is always a sufficient number for normal proceedings, and there is a greater chance of excess than of lack of assistant mediums.

Those invited to participate in the current together with assistant mediums remain seated for many hours in concentration. Is it not tiring?

Apparently yes, but chairs are comfortable and cushioned. Besides, spiritual concentration removes physical weariness entirely.

Do assistant mediums reside in Abadiânia?

Several of them do, but the majority comes from other locations.

16. Opening of procedures and service queues

What happens at the opening of procedures?

From an external perspective works begin in the assembly hall, whereas from an internal perspective one may say that works begin once assistant mediums take their seats.

Where do people about to be submitted to spiritual surgery await their turn?

In the assembly hall, prior to the formation of queues, general announcements are made regarding the procedure for spiritual surgery. Afterwards, those who do not speak Portuguese are guided into a room and those who speak Portuguese enter another room, and in both cases further announcements are made on procedures. They remain seated with eyes closed in concentration, with their thoughts directed to God, without crossing legs, arms, hands, or fingers and with their right hand placed over the sick area or over their hearts.

What is the first-time line?

Those who are visiting Casa de Dom Inácio for the first time are invited to enter this line.

What is the second-time line?

It is made up of people who return to the Casa, be it the second, third or fourth visit.

It must be stated that even if a person has not physically been at the Casa he/she may have been indirectly attended to by means of a photograph or a personal object. If this is the case, despite this first 'visit' in person, a person should enter the second-time line.

What is the 8 am line?

It is made up of people who, according to the Entity, require further spiritual attendance but not surgery. Therefore, in the afternoon it is settled that they have to return by the morning of the following day.

What is the 2 pm line?

It is made up of people whom the Entity asked, in the morning or during the previous day, to return in the afternoon for further spiritual attendance.

How is a person's entrance in queues controlled?

Only people for first-time, second-time, and review lines can pick up line tickets at the bookshop. As soon as they enter the attendance room they must hand over the tickets to a member of staff.

Are service hours rigorously followed?

Attendance to the public takes place in the mornings and in the afternoons, so visitors are advised to be available on such periods. A slightly faster or slower service is not a big problem and Casa visitors do not worry about it.

Which queue is first attended to by the Entity?

The first to receive attendance are those who have a surgery scheduled by the Entity. After that the Entity will state which queue will be attended to next, be it the review line, the first-time or second-time lines, the 8 am or the 2 pm lines. No one knows in advance who will receive attendance after the surgery queue.

Do handicapped visitors have difficulties in lining up?

Difficulties do exist, which are inherent to locomotion deficiency. However people who use both wheelchairs and crutches enter the queues which flow smoothly in the row between the chairs of assistant mediums.

Does Casa de Dom Inácio remain open if a normal day of work coincides with a national or religious holiday?

Yes, and on these days attendance is increased by tour groups and private vehicles. There are also more assistant mediums on such days than available chairs.

The Casa functions normally on Wednesdays, Thursdays, and Fridays, including holidays. When recess occurs, for instance during Christmas or during the medium João's trips abroad, notices are given in advance.

17. Entity services

What happens when a person in line comes face to face with the medium João-in-Entity?

The Entity adopts one of the following procedures when attending a person:

a) tells the person to move on without saying anything or prescribing any medication;

b) hands the person a prescription and tells him/her to move on;

c) hands the person a prescription and invites him/her to take part in the "current";

d) does not prescribe any medication and invites the person to take part in the "current";

e) tells the person to return at 8 am or 2 pm for further spiritual treatment;

f) sets a return date and time for the person to be submitted to spiritual surgery;

g) attends the person immediately by performing spiritual surgery.

Does the medium João-in-Entity remain seated throughout procedures?

Yes, during most of the time of procedures. However he does stand up occasionally when the Entity performs individual spiritual healing. At other times the Entity speaks directly to someone present and passes on a given message.

What is medium João's chair like?

It is a rustic chair, though a comfortable one. It anatomically allows for the relaxation of the body.

When someone seeks a doctor he/she initially offers personal information which is recorded by a secretary, and once the doctor has assessed the patient's condition further information is provided. This common procedure is known as anamnesis[41]. Are such registers made before a person is seen by the Entity?

No, not at all.

Does not the Entity inquire at least a person's name when attending him/her?

No, names have no importance whatsoever. Occasionally the Entity asks where a person lives (city or country) and his/her profession.

One of the possible instructions of the Entity when attending a person is for him/her to sit in the "current". What does this mean?

To sit in the "current" means sitting in one of the chairs of the room where those submitted to spiritual surgery previously stood and forming a "current" of positive thoughts and energies.

The Entity recognizes those who have some degree of mediumship. After attending the person in line, the Entity invites him/her to sit in the "current".

What is the purpose of the recommendation?

The invited person employs his/her mediumship to help in procedures and maintains steady concentration in God and in good spirits.

It is common for the Entity to tell someone who has been attended to "go to work!" What does this mean?

This indeed occurs and it is stated by one of the Entities which incorporate the medium João. It conveys the same meaning as an invitation to sit in the "current".

---

[41] Anamnesis: medical history regarding initial symptoms ascertained in clinical observation. This history is based on a patient's memory.

What happens if someone is invited to sit in the current but does not want to? Can this person refuse the invitation?

Yes.

Vases with flowers are always seen near the chair where the medium João-in-Entity sits. What is the purpose of the flowers?

The flowers are offered by Casa visitors. This happens almost every work day.

Quite often the Entity picks up a flower and offers it to the person who is being attended, whether a man or a woman.

Is it possible for a person to pass by the Entity more than once?

Yes, it is possible, there is no inspection. However there is no point in passing by the Entity more than once during a single day. In addition, the Entity knows if the person has already been attended.

Do people who remain in Abadiânia for weeks or even months pass by the Entity every day?

It depends on the person. One does not have to pass by the Entity every day but there is no prohibition regarding this because a person may feel better simply by going past the Entity, and this happens quite often.

18. Casa colors and white clothes

What are the predominant colors at Casa de Dom Inácio?

White and light blue, both soft colors.

Why is white clothing preferred?

The white color emanates peace and tranquility.

Is the use of white clothing compulsory for Casa visitors?

No, there is only a recommendation for visitors to wear white or some other light-colored clothes. Members of staff and collaborators also follow this recommendation, but it is not an actual rule.

19. Indoor environment

What is the indoor environment at the Casa like?

The mediumistic area is divided into two main parts, an outdoor and an indoor area. The first includes the assembly hall, where short talks are given and queues are formed, whereas the second includes rooms occupied by the medium João-in-Entity and by assistant mediums.

Several people, including the medium João, usually walk barefoot or wear slippers and light shoes without socks. Why?

Unprotected feet assimilate more energy.

Does the environment inside the Casa become warm due to the great number of people who remain inside closed rooms?

No, rooms have air conditioners and many ventilators in order to maintain an adequate temperature.

Quite often an assistant asks mediums to keep their eyes closed and their concentration in God. What is the reason for this?

Eyes closed allow for more effective concentration.

Apart from written notices requesting silence, spoken notices are also given. Why?

Silence is necessary for the concentration of mediums and for efficacy in procedures.

Why is there a recommendation against crossing legs, arms, hands, and fingers?

Legs, arms, hands, and fingers in a normal position enable a person to assimilate energies which flow normally, whereas crossed limbs interrupt this energizing current.

Background music can be heard during the day's works. Is it religious music?

The songs are not necessarily linked to any specific religion, though the themes are indeed religious. It is soft music which makes concentration easier and helps people to relax. The lyrics convey beautiful messages.

20. Medication

Is any medication produced and sold within the Casa complex?
Yes, Passiflora is produced and sold at the Casa.

What is Passiflora?
It consists of capsules which contain passion fruit powder.

Is Passiflora produced only at the Casa?
No, it is also produced elsewhere.

How are the capsules containing passion fruit powder produced?
They are produced in accordance with technical norms under the supervision of a pharmacist.

How are the capsules wrapped?
They are wrapped in recipients of 45 capsules.

Are Passiflora capsules prescribed and sold?
Yes, capsules are distributed only via a prescription given by the Entity. They are sold to those who can afford them and freely given to those who cannot.

How is it possible to know when someone cannot pay for capsules?
The Entity knows it and marks it down on the prescription in order to inform the pharmacist.

Do the industrialization and sale of Passiflora generate profits despite free distribution for those who cannot pay?
Yes.

How are profits from Passiflora sales applied?
Profits are incorporated into the Casa income and used for general maintenance expenses.

21. Photography and filming

Is photography permitted at the Casa?
Yes, when it does not involve commercial purposes. Nevertheless, those interested in photography must solicit authorization in advance and will receive appropriate guidance.

For what reason is there an authorization in advance?

It particularly aims to prevent any kind of interference in the normal conduct of proceedings.

Is authorization for photographing and filming always given?

Not always. When the purpose of photography is mainly commercial authorization may be denied. At other times administrative authorization may be given but the Entity offering services may not allow someone to take photographs.

Why does this occur?

There are Entities that do not identify themselves, just as there are those who do not authorize photography.

What about filming?

The Casa has its own filming service which enables those interested to acquire videos.

What happens in the case of a professional filming session with the aim of producing a documentary film to be released by the press?

In such a case procedures are as follows:

a) authorization by the Entity;

b) agreement on the part of the medium João;

c) preparation of a document by the Casa administration describing the necessary procedures.

The Casa has written norms which are presented to those interested.

Are there stories involving filming and photography for private financial purposes?

Yes, several, for instance there is a documentary film about Casa de Dom Inácio and the medium João recorded in DVD which is currently being sold in another country for over $400 (four hundred dollars). The Casa has no participation in this product's sales and profits.

22. Closing of procedures

Once attendance on queues is concluded, are the period's (morning or afternoon) works finished?

No. There is a standard procedure to be followed in all sessions: once queues have been attended an assistant asks out loud if anyone who has not yet seen the Entity is going to travel and therefore wishes to be attended. Those interested – assistant mediums who helped in procedures – are directed towards the Entity in orderly queues.

How is the closing of procedures conducted?

Once public attendance is over the Entity invites one or more sons and daughters of the Casa to conduct the closing of procedures, which involves a short talk and a prayer.

At the conclusion of works during the morning or the afternoon assistant mediums are invited to drink a cup of fluidified water. What is the reason for this?

The water is energized by spirits who attend the Casa. Fluidified water is part of spiritual treatment and promotes a person's purification. Fluidified water has the same effect as holy water and anoiting oil and its perpetual aim is spiritual purification.

23. Soup distribution

At the end of morning sessions everyone is invited to eat soup which is freely given. How does this work?

In fact every Wednesdays, Thursdays, and Fridays at the end of morning sessions the public is invited to the traditional soup which, like fluidified water, constitutes part of spiritual treatment. Queues proceed normally and everyone is attended without great hassle. Normally a bowl of soup is enough for one person but people may have a second helping or have lunch after the soup if they want to.

Soup expenses are paid by the Casa by means of the income obtained from donations, medication sales, as well as products from the snack bar and the bookshop. The medium João also helps with expenses whenever it is necessary.

How did soup distribution begin?

At the beginning assistant mediums ate lunch at the Casa during breaks between morning and afternoon services on Wednesdays, Thursdays, and Fridays. Many mediums exaggerated on the amount of food and had digestion problems which disturbed their concentration during the afternoon. From then on the Entity settled that mediums should eat light food. Therefore soup began to be prepared initially for assistant mediums only, but was later distributed to members of staff and eventually to all visitors at the Casa.

How many bowls of soup are distributed?

Over 10,000 bowls of soup are distributed at no expense every month for regular Casa visitors or for anyone who goes there in search of food.

24. Casa da Alimentação (Feeding Home)

Apart from the establishment which houses the mediumistic area, does Casa de Dom Inácio own another service area?

Yes, Casa da Alimentação (Feeding Home) at the center of Abadiânia.

What is Casa da Alimentação like?

It is a new building and consists of a kitchen, a dining area, a meeting room, a large hall, an administration room, toilets, changing rooms, a clothing room, and a laundry.

When does soup distribution take place?

On Tuesdays, Wednesdays, and Thursdays, from 10 am to 5 pm, Casa da Alimentação is open and offers soup, tea, and biscuits to anyone.

Anyone, not only poor people?

Yes, no questions are asked regarding a person's financial situation at Casa da Alimentação. All who visit will be served.

Why was Casa da Alimentação opened?

According to the medium João's personal statement, he felt hunger in the past. Therefore he does everything within his power to prevent hunger from afflicting others.

What is the clothing room like?

It is a large hall lined by shelves like any normal shop, on which can be found clothes of all sizes, both male and female items for children and adults.

Are items of clothing sold?

No, clothes are donated to those in need. Anyone who arrives at Casa da Alimentação wearing dirty and worn clothes is free to choose items that fit him/her and wear it. Worn clothing is taken to the laundry to be washed and ironed. Two hours later the person has his/her clothes returned, duly washed, ironed, and wrapped.

Is there a possibility that a person might take advantage of the situation and receive clean clothing without actually needing it?

This has not happened. It seems that a person who is not in need of help will feel ashamed to act in such a dishonest way.

Are donated clothes new or second-hand?

The majority is second-hand and is taken to Casa de Dom Inácio. After having been washed, sterilized, ironed, and conditioned, clothes are stored in the clothing room at Casa da Alimentação.

Is it possible that the stock of clothing may not be sufficient for distribution?

This has not yet occurred. Donations of second-hand clothing and even of new clothing by visitors at Casa de Dom Inácio constitute a reasonable stock. In case of lack of clothing in stock the medium João will personally acquire the necessary clothes for donation.

What is the large hall used for?

The hall is freely lent to anyone wishing to organize a party (eg a birthday party) and has not enough space at home.

Does the medium João feel satisfied with philanthropy performed at the Casa?

No, he always thinks more can be done. He intends to establish a Casa da Alimentação in another location outside Abadiânia.

25. Waterfall baths and crystal baths

How can a waterfall bath be defined?

The waterfall is a natural water spring within Casa grounds. A waterfall bath is a complement of spiritual treatment and it is recommended by the Entity at various moments, at the beginning, in the middle, and at the end of treatment.

What is the name of the stream in which the waterfall lies?

Córrego do Lázaro (Lázaro stream).

How far is the Casa from the waterfall?

Approximately 1 km.

Does a person have to pay for a waterfall bath?

No.

Is the waterfall free for all comers?

No, access to the waterfall is restricted. Only those sent by the Entity may enter the waterfall area.

What is a crystal bath?

In an appropriate room within the Casa there is a table/bed the size of a single bed and there are many crystal-covered lights shining down on an individual lying down on this bed. Those interested may have a crystal bath, which involves lying down on the table for no longer than 20 minutes because of the intense energetic environment.

What is the purpose of the crystal bath?

To provide energy. The crystal bath aims to offer cleansing, spiritual peace, and balance for the chakras of the human body.

26. Communication

Are Portuguese courses for foreigners offered in Abadiânia?

Yes, such courses are offered sporadically and have no connection with the Casa. However the stay in Abadiânia is usually quite short, so it is not possible for foreign visitors to learn Portuguese. All that is offered are basic communication tips.

In most inns there are people who communicate well in English and some even speak German, French, and Spanish. Several foreign visitors try to learn some Portuguese before traveling to Abadiânia, whereas others visit Abadiânia regularly and are gradually able to communicate in Portuguese. Nevertheless, there are many interpreters at the Casa.

People from several countries seek Casa de Dom Inácio and naturally use the local taxis. How does communication occur?

Even though taxi drivers are humble people, the majority speaks enough English to establish communication.

Are there English courses in Abadiânia for those wishing to improve communication with foreigners?

Yes.

27. Income and expenses

How are the Casa's income and expenses calculated?

In two ways: the first accountancy is carried out by a worker who is in charge of registering workers, INSS, FGTS[*], hiring, resignations, bookshop purchases and sales, snack bar, and pharmacy (Passiflora); the following accountancy is carried out by the Casa's own administration regarding donations. Both accountancies aim at maintaining, functioning, and balancing finances (income/expense).

Are prices at the snack bar and at the bookshop higher than those found in local commerce in general?

No, prices are similar to those of any other snack bar or bookshop. Some products are cheaper.

Apart from profits obtained by the bookshop and the snack bar, are there other sources of income?

Yes, the sale of Passiflora and donations.

---

[*]Brazilian pay roll contributions – T.N.

Does Casa de Dom Inácio receive many donations?

Yes, donations are placed in collecting boxes found at the bookshop, at the snack bar, and in the assembly hall. No member of staff is authorized to receive donations.

How are donations made?

In the manner that a person chooses: in Brazilian reais, in checks, in dollars, or some other foreign currency which will be exchanged. Donations are placed inside appropriate boxes and are not to be given directly to a member of staff.

Are donations anonymous?

Generally yes. People feel free to place donations inside collecting boxes without identifying themselves. However, if the donator requests a receipt he/she may hand the donation directly to the Administrator and make the request.

Are donations freely given or is there some norm regulating them?

The word "donation" itself says it all: it may be given by anyone who wishes, if, when, and how much they wish to give.

28. Other information

Are mediumistic services in Abadiânia free?

Yes, totally free.

Are people allowed to use cellular phones at the Casa?

Not inside the assistant mediums' rooms or in the queues so as not to disturb concentration.

Are baptisms performed at the Casa?

Yes, there is a specific ritual for baptisms. They are not conducted by the medium João but by volunteers who know the procedures.

Will any person who wishes to talk to the medium João as himself be attended to?

In theory yes. Occasionally the Entity tells someone from a queue to talk to the medium João at the end of procedures. These people are attended on a regular basis.

The majority mixes up the medium João with the Entity and wishes to talk to him. It is extremely difficult for the medium João to attend all visitors, so he does his best to see as many as possible.

Apparently everything that goes on at Casa de Dom Inácio is related to the medium João. What will happen after his death?

According to him, the Casa will continue to work.

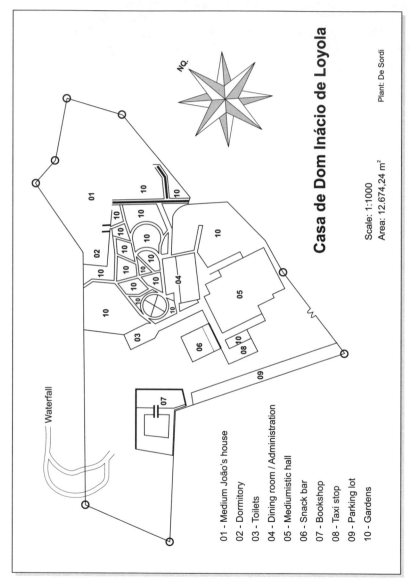

Casa de Dom Inácio de Loyola

NQ.

Waterfall

01 - Medium João's house
02 - Dormitory
03 - Toilets
04 - Dining room / Administration
05 - Mediumistic hall
06 - Snack bar
07 - Bookshop
08 - Taxi stop
09 - Parking lot
10 - Gardens

Scale: 1:1000
Area: 12.674,24 m²

Plant: De Sordi

Figure 1 – Casa de Dom Inácio (physical space)

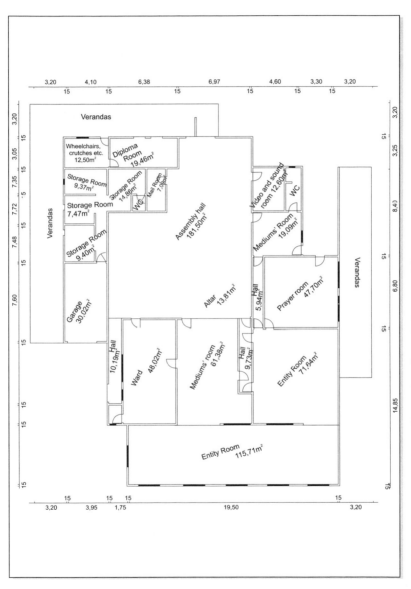

Figure 2 – Casa de Dom Inácio (mediumistic area)

Chapter IV

Entities

The number of visitors who wishes to find out as much as possible about the spiritual manifestations which take place at Casa de Dom Inácio is always considerable. This chapter presents some information regarding the Entities incorporated by the medium João.

1. Initial comments

Is it over pretentious to state that some of the answers presented in this book were provided by interviewed spirits?

It depends from what angle the matter is viewed. To many this sounds like fantasy or a thoughtless joke: how are we to believe that questions are answered by the spirit of a person who lived many centuries ago? However, the author is not concerned with whether the reader believes it or not, all he does is report facts. It is up to the reader to make deductions and arrive at the conclusions which suit him/her best.

Can any person speak to the Entity?

Yes, people can and do in fact speak to the Entity. Every person who is lined up and seen by the medium João is in fact seen by the Entity who incorporates the medium at a particular moment. The Entity listens more than speaks and it seldom asks questions. However, people may question the Entity and say what they wish.

Is it common for people to speak to the Entity while they are being attended to?

The majority does not speak at all especially due to their intense emotional state. Some people cry, ask questions, and express thanks, but only a few discuss their problems in detail.

2. Incorporation and de-incorporation

In which particular moment does incorporation in the medium João occur?

In a closed room, an assistant in procedures asks mediums to reinforce concentration by closing their eyes. The medium João enters the room, says a prayer, and places himself at the disposal of good spirits as an instrument for the practice of good. Incorporation takes place at this moment, and it happens in public, in the presence of the assistant mediums.

When does de-incorporation occur?

Once people in queues and assistant mediums who wish to pass by the Entity are attended to, two sons or daughters of the Casa are designated to conduct the closing of procedures. Soon afterwards the medium João, already de-incorporated, retires to the rest room.

Why do other mediums with similar abilities to those of the medium João normally incorporate only one spirit while he incorporates several?

The author does not have an answer to this question. According to the medium João himself, this aspect constitutes part of his mission.[42]

How can one tell if a person is speaking to the medium João himself or to João-in-Entity?

One cannot tell. Nevertheless, one knows that the medium João is incorporated during attendance to the queues. Only a few who possess more experience and greater mediumistic knowledge are able to state when the medium João is incorporated or not.

3. Entities

Is it possible to identify the Entity that is offering services?

The Entity identifies itself occasionally. Some regular visitors are able to recognize certain Entities by paying attention to the medium's João voice, his way of walking, and his manners. Other Entities do not identify themselves or are not identified.

How many spirits incorporate in the medium João?

Several, as was previously answered by the medium himself in Chapter II, n. 4.

How many spirits are incorporated by the medium João in one day, on average?

There is no concern over such number, it is not important.

---

[42] See Chapter II, n. 4.

Are some spirits more often present than others?

Yes. The most famous Entities who work at the Casa are: Doctor Augusto de Almeida, Doctor José Valdivino, Saint Francis Xavier, Saint Ignatius of Loyola, Osvaldo Cruz, King Solomon, Bezerra de Menezes, Sister Scheilla, André Luiz, and Eurípedes Barsanulfo.

How many spirits are present at Casa de Dom Inácio in addition to those who incorporate in the medium João?

It is difficult to tell. It is said that each Entity has a "phalange" of assistant spirits. On one of the walls at the Casa there is a portrait of Augusto de Almeida – one of the Entities incorporated by the medium João –, on which the following words can be read: "It is not dozens or hundreds of spirits who accompany me, but thousands".

It is said that the medium Joao is incorporated by several Entities. Is it possible to know when there is a change from one Entity to another?

No.

4. Communication

Does the Entity communicate in other languages other than Portuguese?

No.

If the Entity knows all, why does it not establish communication in other languages and make the presence of interpreters unnecessary?

The author is not able to answer this question.

5. Infiltration and Identification

Has the Entity ever expressed the reason for a person's visit and identified this visitor?

More often than people think. Visitors are often recognized.

Is the identification by an Entity straightforward?

Yes.

Does this happen often?

There are several stories on this regard. The author is acquainted with a police chief whose job was to investigate and close the Casa if necessary. While he was being attended to the Entity identified him and revealed the reason for his visit. The Entity told him to observe procedures and only then take the measures he considered suitable.

What happened after this episode?

The police chief started to attend regularly and was declared a son of the Casa.

Are there reports on embarrassing cases of identification of the motive of a person's visit which did not involve spiritual healing?

Yes. The author once witnessed an episode in which the Entity told the person being attended to that she had sought the wrong place, because she would not be able to perform a "despacho"* in order to "hold on" to her lover. This person did not express the reason for her visit in advance.

Another episode may be registered as well, which involved a journalist. On one occasion the Entity said that a given person who was sitting amidst the assistant mediums, on a given row and chair and wearing certain clothes, was a journalist and that he/she was there to collect information for a report. The journalist was a foreigner and spoke reasonable Portuguese. Without approaching, the Entity invited the journalist out loud to step forward and observe the procedure closely, as well as photograph and film whatever he/she deemed important in order to fulfill the reason for the visit as naturally as possible.

6. Famous Entities

In specific terms, which are the most well-known Entities incorporated by the medium João?

The names of some Entities are well-known and there is a vast historical reference about them. Others identify themselves but no information

---

* Word for 'witchcraft' associated with the Macumba, a Brazilian religion of African origins. The word 'macumba' and rituals connected with it are widely regarded as pejorative and offensive among the majority of Brazilians. – T.N.

can be found on who they actually were when incarnated. Finally, there are many who do not identify themselves and prefer to preserve their anonymity.

The following brief biographies were obtained through several sources.

SAINT IGNATIUS OF LOYOLA

St. Ignatius of Loyola was born in 1491 in the Basque region of Guipúzcoa, Spain. At the baptismal font he was named Iñigo López de Oñaz y Loyola.

Some biographers divide his life into four distinct phases, as follows:

First phase – Mundane concerns: a son of an illustrious family, Iñigo was a handsome and intelligent young man who spent his youth in the court of Castilha as a nobleman and a knight. During this period he was overpowered by a bellicose temper which distinguished him for his courage, bravery, and noble deeds. As a military commander in the war against France, while he promoted the defense of the city of Pamplona, he was wounded by a cannon ball and one of his legs was broken and the other badly wounded. The fortress where he fought was eventually captured by French troops. He was arrested and released together with his soldiers in honor of his nobility and bravery. A surgery was carried out in order to re-shape his leg, and this almost drove him to death – the final sacraments were in fact performed for him. As a result of the surgery he became limp.

Second phase – Spiritual reorientation: in the hope of eliminating physical handicap, Iñigo was submitted to a second and equally painful surgery. He read extensively during his convalescence. The only books he found in the castle concerned the life of Christ and the lives of saints. He gradually underwent a change and began to despise material riches and abandon previous thoughts of greatness and reminiscences of happy days spent at court. He began to meditate increasingly about life and gradually heightened his spirituality. Iñigo left his family, embraced faith definitively, and exchanged his noble garments for humble clothes. The former valiant captain turned into a beggar and from this moment on, his spirituality only grew. He suffered great humiliation and was nicknamed "brother of the sack" because of his clothing. The generosity of his conduct attracted the attention of people, who began to consult with him and ask for his advice. Thus his apostolate began.

Third phase – Late fulfillment of religious studies: at first in Barcelona and later in Salamanca, Iñigo dedicated his time to studies, preachings, and the conversion of sinners. He was arrested and sued by the Inquisition and subsequently acquitted and permitted to preach to the people. He traveled to Paris with the aim of pursuing his studies. There he Latinized his name to Ignatius and received a degree of master. Still in Paris, he was able to bring together a group of companions, among them Peter Faber, Francis Xavier, and Diogo Lanez.

Fourth phase – Founding of the Society of Jesus: Ignatius' sanctity spread rapidly especially among young people, who sought him for spiritual guidance. Supported by this group of followers he founded the first community in 1534, known as the Society of Jesus (a Jesuit order). He possessed a healing gift and performed incredible prodigies to those who sought his spiritual and temporal aid. His disciples organized preachings in public squares in many Italian cities. In 1540, after many years, the Society of Jesus finally received approval as a religious order by Pope Paul III. Ignatius performed intense apostolic work, multiplied religious houses, and initiated missionaries in all continents and even in Brazil, in whose history the Society of Jesus held a central position under the direction of the priest Manoel da Nóbrega.

Ignatius of Loyola died in Rome in 1556.[43]

AUGUSTO DE ALMEIDA

Little is known regarding Augusto de Almeida. The medium João states that he knows him from past lives and that he was a military officer, a doctor, and a rubber tapper. The spirit of Augusto de Almeida is one of the most frequently incorporated Entities at the Casa. He is easily recognized for his strict and occasionally harsh manners, a true military attitude. He is easily identified by the oldest visitors of the Casa by authoritative attitudes which demand great discipline on the part of those who assist him in procedures.

During his incarnation as a doctor Augusto witnessed great suffering because anesthesia had not been invented at the time. He operated on patients who endured pain by biting on a piece of cloth. On account of such suffering he started to dedicate efforts to relieve the pain of those who seek Casa de Dom Inácio, where he performs cures, surgeries, and prescribes medication.

---

[43] Saint Ignatius of Loyola: http://planetaterra.com.br/arte/sfv/StInacio.html. Accessed: jan 11 2005.

Dr. Augusto is extremely just, performs his work with a serious manner, and does not admit interruptions during attendance to the public.

ΙJOSÉ VALDIVINO

No one knows exactly who he was when incarnated. He is friendly, affectionate, closely linked to family affairs, and extremely helpful to those he attends. The medium João believes José Valdivino was a legal judge during his life.

ΙSAINT FRANCIS XAVIER

Francisco de Jassu y Javier was born in 1506, at the Castle of Javier, close to the city of Pamplona in Spain. He was born to a noble family, rich in material possessions and honorific titles, and grew up among riches and traditions. From an early age he revealed great intelligence and dedication to studies. He studied in Paris from the age of 19 to 28 at the College of St. Barbara, where he was Peter Faber's roommate. Peter's friendship proved very beneficial for Francis' impulsive temperament. While in Paris he met Calvin, who later helped to establish the Protestant Reformation in Europe. It was also at the College of St. Barbara that Francis Xavier met Ignatius of Loyola, with whom he became close friends and from whom he received religious teachings and financial aid when family support ceased.

He graduated in Philosophy in 1526 and received the degree of master (professor) in 1530. On August 15, 1534, under the leadership of Ignatius of Loyola, Francis, Peter Faber, and four other friends made vows of poverty and chastity and were the first Jesuits and future founders of the Society of Jesus. Xavier went on to preach in India, Japan, and in other Eastern nations.

Francis Xavier died at the age of 46 on December 3, 1552, at Shangchuan Island off the coast of China, after having traveled over 120,000 km converting and baptizing thousands of pagans. Despite the considerable amount of chalk placed inside his coffin for a quick decomposition of the body – which would allow only his bones to be transported back at the unearthing and opening of the coffin 3 months later –, his friends were surprised and amazed to find that there was no smell and that the body remained in perfect condition. The body was taken to Malaga and then to Goa, where it remains to this day at the Basilica of Bom Jesus and is a daily shrine for the devotion of worshippers. He performed several unexplainable cures during his life and many miracles are attributed to his intercession because he attended to prayers that were performed in the presence of his body.

Francis Xavier wrote wonderful letters which were copied and distributed by Ignatius of Loyola. Such letters used to be read in churches because they inspired vocations and revealed to people the extraordinary example of his life.

He was canonized on March 12, 1622 and is regarded as the great Apostle of modern times just as St. Paul was the notable Apostle of ancient times. He was proclaimed the universal patron of missions by Pope Pius XI and is widely regarded as the greatest of all missionaries.[44]

OSVALDO CRUZ

Osvaldo Cruz was born in São Luiz do Paraitinga, São Paulo, in 1872. He was extremely intelligent and by the age of 5 was already able to read and write. His family moved to Rio de Janeiro in 1877. He was admitted into Medicine School when he was 15 years old. As a student he published two works on microbiology. In 1892, at the age of 20, he concluded Medicine School with the thesis entitled *A Veiculação Microbiana Pela Água* (Microbial Transport Through Water) which was approved with honors. In 1893 he married Emília Fonseca, a woman of a traditional family of Rio de Janeiro, with whom he had six children.

In 1896 Osvaldo Cruz traveled to France and was accepted into the Pasteur Institute, where he worked for 3 years. He was admired by his professors because of his intelligence and his dedication to microbiology. In 1899, despite the Institute's invitation for him to remain in Paris, he returned to Brazil and expressed revolt against the pejorative international propaganda: "Brazil is a vast hospital". He accepted the invitation to direct the Institute of Hygiene and thus assess and fight the pest which thrived at Santos' harbor.

After the founding of the Federal Serotherapy Institute located at Manguinhos Farm, in the outskirts of Rio de Janeiro, the Brazilian government asked the directors of the Pasteur Institute to recommend and offer one of its collaborators to lead Brazil's project of vaccine production. As an answer they were informed that one of its most qualified technicians lived in Rio de Janeiro and was called Osvaldo Cruz.

---

[44] *A Vida de São Francisco Xavier*. Available at: http://apostolado.sites.uol.com.br/morxa.htm. Accessed: oct 25 2005.

In 1900 Cruz accepted the invitation to run the Manguinhos Institute, now known as Osvaldo Cruz Foundation (Fiocruz). He developed an intensive campaign of compulsory vaccination and effective protection against yellow fever, mosquitoes, and rats. Compulsory vaccination – with its famous "kill-mosquitoes" brigades – rendered him fierce opposition, which he fought with great tenacity.

In 1910 Cruz was invited to perform sanitary studies in the states of Amazonas (Madeira-Mamoré railroad) and Pará (Belém). In 1912 he headed sanitation programs in the Amazon Valley.

Cruz received several national and international awards and was even elected for the Brazilian Academy of Letters.

Sick and exhausted, he retired to the city of Petrópolis in 1916, where he was elected mayor. However he renounced before completing his mandate because his private affairs had been disturbed in virtue of his tendency of attributing priority to the greater good.

He died in 1917 before reaching the age of 45. He left as inheritance a foundation which produced 60% of vaccines worldwide.

KING SOLOMON

Solomon was the second son of King David. He ruled Israel for forty years (970 – 930 BC) according to biblical accounts. As a ruler he was notorious for his administrative competence: he built roads and intensified commerce which spread to distant corners of his kingdom. Even though he had powerful armies at his command, he preferred to establish commerce than to go to war and possessed an extreme ability to maintain peace and to avoid conflicts.

Solomon possessed a cosmic awareness and perfectly distinguished negative and positive forces present in the knowledge acquired through meditation. Therefore, free will would allow the use of positive knowledge. Thus he abandoned the use of negative interests and directed his mind to the good side of knowledge.

Despite the great aura of legend surrounding them, the so-called "Mines of King Solomon" offered all the necessary riches for a sumptuous government. Intensive archeological research have discovered traces of a city-fortress in the middle of the African forest with abandoned mines in the surroundings, and such a discovery provides evidence that this may have been the wealthy lost city of Ofir, from whence considerable amounts of gold were sent to Solomon.

He is an important figure in the history of Masonry and the temple he built serves as a symbolic base.

In historical terms he is known for his sense of justice. The expression "Justice of Solomon" is widespread and refers to what is due to a person. The episode of Solomon's judgement involving the dispute of two women over the maternity of a child is notorious. In order to solve the mystery Solomon ordered that the child be cut in half and each part be given to each of the pretense mothers. The true mother then begged for the child's life and allowed him to be given to the other woman. Solomon wisely decided that the child should be given to the former because only a true mother would renounce her right of maternity to another person in order to preserve her child's life.

The biblical books of *Proverbs*, *Canticle of Canticles*, and *Ecclesiastes* are attributed to King Solomon.

BEZERRA DE MENEZES

Bezerra de Menezes' full name is Adolfo Bezerra de Menezes Cavalcanti. He was born in Freguesia do Riacho do Sangue, present-day Jaguaretama, Ceará State, on August 29, 1831. He was a friar, a professor, a doctor, a military officer, a politician, a businessman, and a writer.

Despite being a wealthy man, his father jeopardized his fortune by helping others. He left honor and steady character as inheritance for his son. As a result, Bezerra de Menezes suffered material hardships but he was always ready to give what he had to those in need. Initially a Catholic, Menezes converted to Spiritism after reading Allan Kardec's *The Spirits' Book*.

On one occasion, while he attended Medicine School and underwent serious financial difficulties, he was in urgent need of 50,000 réis (the Brazilian currency at the time) in order to pay several debts, including rent, and faced the threat of eviction. He turned to God in desperation. A few days later a pleasant and polite young man turned up at his door with the wish of taking math lessons. Menezes hated this subject, but ended up accepting the offer due to his desperate financial situation and the young man's insistence, and he reluctantly agreed to receive payment for all lessons in advance in a total of 50,000 réis. Menezes paid everything he owed and studied a great deal in preparation for the lessons. However, the young man never returned. Years later, during a Spiritist session, he was encouraged to offer more assistance to those in spiritual need. He pointed out that he needed to earn his living and had no means of solely dedicating to Spiritism. At that moment the medium who incorporated St. Augustine stated, "we will help you by bringing you new math pupils when necessary."

Menezes' following statement represents his professional attitude:

A doctor does not have the right to finish a meal nor to inquire if a place is near or far when an afflicted person knocks at his door. A doctor who does not offer assistance because of visits, excessive tiredness, because of the lateness of the hour, bad road or weather, distance, who asks for a car to someone who cannot pay for the prescription or tells someone who cries at his door to seek another, is not a doctor but a businessman of Medicine.

Bezerra de Menezes was known as the "doctor of the poor" because of his dedication and charitable spirit. He was the president of the Brazilian Spiritist Federation for several years and earned the title of "Brazilian Kardec" for all his good deeds. He died on April 11, 1900.[45]

ANDRÉ LUIZ

André Luiz is not his real name and little is known about him. All that is known is that he worked as a doctor in Rio de Janeiro in the early 20th century. Some argue that he may have been Carlos Chagas but such hypotheses are no more than mere deductions. He revealed a rich and vast contribution from the spiritual domain and several of his books were psychographed by Francisco Cândido Xavier. His first and most famous book was *Nosso Lar* (translated into English as *The Astral City*), which was published in 1944. Among the books he dictated are *Os Mensageiros* (The Messengers), *Missionários da Luz* (Missionaries of the Light), *Obreiros da Vida Eterna* (Workers of Eternal Life), *No Mundo Maior* (In the Wider World), *Ação e Reação* (Action and Reaction), *Libertação* (Liberation), *Entre a Terra e o Céu* (Between Earth and Sky), *Domínios da Mediunidade* (In The Domain of Mediumship), *Mecanismo da Mediunidade* (Mechanism of Mediumship), *Conduta Espírita* (Spiritual Conduct), *Sol nas Almas* (Sun in Souls) and *Endereços da Paz* (Addresses of Peace).[46]

---

[45] http://www.feparana.com.br/biografias/adolfo-bezerra.htm. Accessed: jan 11 2005.
[46] André Luiz - Perfil e Obras - http://www.geocities.com/Paris/Power/1120/andre.htm. Accessed: jan 14 2005.

｜*SISTER SCHEILLA*

Sister Scheilla was born in Germany. She was a nurse and aided victims during the Second World War. She died in July or August of 1943 during violent air raids.

It is reported that in a previous life she lived in France with the name Jeanne Françoise Frémiot. She was born in Dijon on January 28, 1572 and died in Moulins on December 13, 1641. During her French existence she worked intensely for social assistance and was canonized in 1767 as Saint Joan of Chantal.

The spirit of Sister Scheilla is particularly known for attendance on sick people. Her presence is noted at the Casa by a perfumed scent in the room.

｜*EMMANUEL*

Emmanuel is especially well-known because he was Chico Xavier's spiritual mentor. It is widely known that he was the proud Roman senator Publius Lentulus 2,000 years ago, who lived for Caesar and to Caesar surrounded by luxury and ostentation. From the tribune of Circus Maximus he witnessed the execution of Livia, the wife he loved, because of her conversion to Christianity. He disincarnated in Pompey in the year 79 AD at the eruption of the Vesuvius.

His spirit began to rescue past failures in the search for evolution and reincarnated as the slave Nestorio fifty years later. Nestorio died in a Roman arena together with Christian elderly people, youths, and children, who served as a public spectacle by being devoured by beasts.

Approximately 150 years later he returned to Earth as Roman patrician Quinto Varro who assumed the identity of an old preacher named Corvino in order to escape a conspiracy to kill him. After being convicted for beheading, he was granted a slow death in jail.

Several centuries passed before he reincarnated once again in 1517 in Portugal as the priest Manuel da Nóbrega. Nóbrega was one of the main figures of the Society of Jesus founded by Ignatius of Loyola and played a prominent role in the history of Brazil through the founding of Colégio Piratininga (Piratininga College), which was the birthplace of the great metropolis of São Paulo. He died of tuberculosis in Rio de Janeiro at the age of 53.

As far as the spelling of Emmanuel - not Manuel – is concerned, there is evidence pointing to the name E. Manuel (as in Ermano Manuel) as was signed by Manuel da Nóbrega.[47]

| EURÍPEDES BARSANULFO

Eurípedes Barsanulfo was born on May 1, 1880, in the town of Sacramento, Minas Gerais. He possessed keen intelligence and was an educator from an early age. He was designated by his professor to teach his own classmates. Because of his undisputable sense of leadership he went on to occupy the post of secretary of the brotherhood of Saint Vincent de Paul. He was an autodidact and worked as a professor of several subjects, as a journalist, and as a politician.

He became familiar with the works of codifier Allan Kardec through his uncle. He read about the new doctrine intensely, increased his knowledge on the subject, and converted to Spiritism. As a result of this conversion he was misunderstood by relatives and friends. Fearlessly he included Spiritism in the school syllabus, which rendered him strong opposition and an exodus of students from school promoted by their parents.

Having become traumatized because of countless misunderstandings and persecutions Barsanulfo retired from his activities and sought treatment and recovery. During this period he revealed various mediumistic abilities, especially healing. His own mother was one of the first people to benefit from cures performed through his mediation. The town of Sacramento became a peregrination center for people who sought some sort of relief from physical and psychological ailments. Eurípedes Barsanulfo attended all who went to see him with joy and dedication.

His spiritual activities continually increased and he felt the need to make the new doctrine known and to increase the number of followers. With support from some relatives and friends Barsanulfo founded the Hope and Charity Spiritist Center, which resulted in the intensification of doctrinary and assistential work. Physically he was skinny but good-looking and he was not found wanting in marriage proposals. However he declared that he could never get married because he was already married to "poverty".

In 1907 Barsanulfo founded the Allan Kardec School which became a model educational institution in the region and subsequently in the whole

---

[47] Emmanuel. Available at: http://www.ame.org.br/emmanuel.htm. Accessed: jan 14 2005.

of Brazil. The number of people seeking the school was so great that there were no more vacancies at the end of the first day of applications. The school was forced to close its doors for some time due to the epidemic of Spanish influenza.

On one occasion he fell into a trance in the middle of the classroom. When he regained his senses he provided a detailed account and mentioned the names of participants and the appointed hours for the meeting held at the Palace of Versailles soon after the end of World War I.

Barsanulfo did not seek religious confrontation but on one occasion humbly accepted a challenge of public debate with a representative of the Catholic Church. His performance was brilliant in every aspect, having preached love, tolerance, and charity. As a result his social status grew even more. This also occurred when a criminal lawsuit filed against him was closed.[48]

All his energies were spent in assisting the victims (especially the poor) of the worldwide Spanish influenza epidemic and their relatives.

On November 1, 1918, exhausted by his efforts, he died surrounded by relatives, friends, and admirers.[49]

Which other Entities can be identified despite lack of reference regarding their incarnations?

The following Entities may be cited:

José: the identification is limited to "I am José" (it is not the spirit of José Valdivino);

Terezinha D'Ávila: all that is known is that she was a nun and is not Saint Teresa of Avila;

Amor (Love): when questioned about its identity the Entity answers that its name is "Amor" (Love).

Are there spirits who identify themselves but are not well-known?

Yes. There is the curious case of a spirit who periodically attends at the Casa and identifies itself. At the end of procedures nobody is able to tell what the identification given was.

---

[48] See also Chapter VI, n. 17.

[49] Eurípedes Barsanulfo. Available at: http://www.ceismael.com.br/bio/bio08.htm. Accessed: jan 11 2005.

Why do several Entities fail to identify themselves?

The author is unable to explain this. Such Entities simply consider identification irrelevant.

The identification of the spirit is least important. What matters is the quality of the performed procedure.

Chapter V

Spiritual Cures

This chapter has the same title as this book and reports in general terms what happens at Casa de Dom Inácio, though it does not intend to explain "how" or "why" certain facts occur. First of all some general considerations regarding spiritual healing are made, followed by forty accounts of real healing cases.

1. Initial measures

What were the initial measures for the development of this chapter?

The author's main concern was to present a reasonable number of spiritual cures performed at Casa de Dom Inácio. He considered it best to mention a great deal of information regarding benefited individuals, so reports include people's names and addresses, health problems, treatments, and obtained cures.

Why does the chapter begin with general comments on spiritual cures and is not limited to real healing accounts?

Because readers will have access to information concerning details of spiritual cures and will henceforth draw their own conclusions without interference from others.

For what reason are the addresses of spiritually healed individuals provided?

Those interested in confirming spiritual cures may get in touch with any of the people hereby listed through the stated addresses and these will certainly be able to provide further details on the cures they received. Telephone numbers are not provided in order to prevent unnecessary problems and also because they eventually change.

2. Frauds in spiritual healing

Are there frauds and simulations in spiritual treatments?

Yes, several.

Do the words 'healer' and 'healing medium' convey the same meaning?

Specialists on the subject state that there are differences between these terms. A healer is a person who possesses energy capable of performing cures. On the other hand, a medium is only an instrument which is dominated by a spirit. Healing is performed by the spirit, not by the medium, hence spiritual healing. An individual may be a 'healer' but not a healing medium. The activity of the healer almost always equates with healing, whereas healing mediumship is a divine mission which is still scientifically unexplainable. Nevertheless, it is a polemic subject and requires further scientific research.

How can a non-specialist tell the difference between them?

It is not easy. Normally the healer charges for services, but the healing medium does not. A healer uses his/her activity as a means to earn a living, whereas the healing medium only performs the activity as a divine mission. Healing usually involves cons, whereas frauds are rare in healing mediumship.

Is it common to find people who are healing mediums?

One needs to establish a distinction between mediums who perform spiritual healing through prayers and passes and incorporated mediums who perform spiritual surgeries, occasionally involving cuts.

Are healing mediums who perform spiritual surgeries with cuts rare?

From time to time someone with special abilities comes along, who serves as an apparatus for spiritual healing by establishing contact with a sick person. Occasionally surgery interventions are made without assepsis, anesthesia, and pain in a way that still defies conventional medicine. Quite often scars are seen but cannot be scientifically explained. Even though nothing is externally visible, the surgery itself is performed internally.

There are no precise statistics available, but it is estimated that one medium appears among millions and millions of people and through this individual spiritual surgeries involving cuts are performed.

Which healing mediums like João de Deus are known in Brazil?

Several, the most well-known are Zé Arigó and Edson Queiroz.

Have scientific, police, or journalistic investigations been carried out in the past with the aim of verifying the existence of frauds in spiritual cures performed through the medium João?

Yes. Several scientific investigations have been carried out, especially by foreign researchers, as well as various police inquests against the medium João, and journalistic investigations carried out by many professionals in order to support press reports.

108

Were such journalistic researches superficial or detailed?

There were some detailed investigations organized by competent journalists and divulged by companies which enjoy great credibility with the public opinion worldwide. The author prefers not to mention any names.

How is one to accept the fact that there are no frauds related to the medium João?

A fraud involving millions of people is impossible. It is not possible to deceive people for more than 25 years, which is the period during which Casa de Dom Inácio has been active. This does not take into account the period during which the medium João continually attended thousands of people in different locations.

Is the medium João a thaumaturge, in other words, a person who performs miracles?

Absolutely not. The medium João does not heal anyone, he only serves as an instrument for good spirits.

3. Procedures in spiritual healing

In what consist spiritual healing performed through the mediation of the medium João?

Such procedures may or may not involve physical contact. Spiritual cures devoid of physical contact consist of prayers and invisible surgery.

Is the healing procedure always the same at Casa de Dom Inácio?

It is nearly always the same. The first step is the initial consultation with spiritual Entities which indicate how attendance should occur. There are no miracles or magic tricks because everything depends on faith and merit.

Are procedures for spiritual healing simple or complex?

They may appear simple to those who observe only from the outside, whereas Medicine professionals regard them as anything but straightforward.

4. Attendance in spiritual healing

Is it not more appropriate to employ the term 'spiritual treatment' instead of 'spiritual healing'?

It depends on the point of view from which the subject is analyzed. All those who go to Casa de Dom Inácio receive spiritual treatment, but spiritual healing is not always achieved by everyone.

Is a person free to choose a certain type of attendance?

No, it is the Entity who decides.

Depending on a person's cultural background, is it possible to be psychologically influenced?

Yes, it seems that way. In order to confirm a given cure – and taking into account the widespread belief that uneducated people are easily influenced – a simulation is less easily believed when the benefited person has a higher cultural standard.

Are there individuals of a higher cultural standard among those benefited by spiritual cures performed through the medium João?

Yes. Individuals who benefited from spiritual cures include lawyers, engineers, doctors, psychologists, liberal professionals of various fields, university professors, officers from the Armed Forces, politicians, artists, and businessmen, therefore, people with solid intellectual background.

How many people are attended every day, on average?

All those present are attended to, both in the morning and in the afternoon. There are no limits as to number.

How many are healed?

Nobody knows. Healing may be physical or spiritual. Several factors may prevent healing from taking place, especially lack of merit and conduct after attendance. However, everybody receives some sort of benefit.

Does the fact that a person is spiritually operated on means that he/she is cured?

Not always, it depends on each person's merit. Countless benefited people had their physical health altered. However, the most important change concerns spiritual health.

What is merit?

Merit consists in spiritual conditions that were accumulated in past incarnations and that may be added to one's present conduct in order for a person to be deserving of intended healing. An individual must improve his/her soul in order to obtain merit. When a person has earned merit, he/she will find the cure in any place and in any religion.

Is faith sufficient for obtaining spiritual healing?

Yes, but in the author's opinion it must be accompanied by a spiritual conduct which warrants merit.

What happens if a person does not have faith or does not believe in the positive result of the prescribed medication or in the performed spiritual cure?

If a person deserves benefits the outcome will be positive, be it through spiritual surgery or only through medication.

Does spiritual surgery involve risks?

It is not the spiritual surgery which produces negative outcomes, but the illness that was not removed despite spiritual treatment. Even if the intended benefit fails to occur there will be no negative results. Any surgery performed by conventional medicine involves risks, but when frauds do not take place there are no such risks in spiritual surgeries.

Are there errors in spiritual treatments?

No, good spirits do not make mistakes. Even though there are no errors, the medium João has been criminally sued several times and responsibility will be attributed to him, as the instrument of spirits, if such errors actually occur.

Medical errors do occur in conventional treatments. Why are there no errors in spiritual treatments?

Doctors are humans, and to err is human. Good spirits know what they are doing. Spiritual medicine is very much superior to human medicine.

Mistakes only occur when there are frauds in attendance and in treatment. If the spiritual service is seriously performed then mistakes will not occur.

Who may receive spiritual cures?

Any person, as long as one warrants merit. If a person deserves to receive spiritual healing then no questions are asked regarding sex, age, color, religion, nationality, cultural background or economic situation, because there is no discrimination whatsoever. Healing begins with self-knowledge.

Is long distance healing possible?

Yes, accounts of people who received long distance treatments are common. One possible way of treatment at a distance occurs when the Entity examines photographs, items of clothing or objects of absent people and prescribes medication for them. It is also quite usual for the Entity to state that he/she will visit the absent person, no matter where or how far they are.

Is spiritual healing solely aimed at physical illnesses?

No. Even though there are no real statistics concerning the matter, it seems that moral effects and psychological cures, all of which offer spiritual peace, occur more frequently.

In general terms, how does the spirit detect a person's physical problem?

The perispirit of the attended person is revealed as a type of x-ray, so it shows what is not well.

How can spiritual healing be scientifically explained?

As far as the author's scarce knowledge is concerned, quite a lot of what happens cannot be scientifically explained. He registers the following points from his intensive reading:

- it is not only the body that is prone to illness, so the spirit must also receive treatment;
- those who have faith respond better to any treatment, an opinion shared by both science and religion;
- it is not possible to heal those who do not wish to be healed: where there is a will, there is a way;
- each person possesses an internal motor, a "divine spark" that leads to cure.

For what reason does the Entity refrain from telling a person directly that he/she will be cured or not?

The author is not able to answer this question. One knows that the Entity does not say "I will heal you!" What is always stated is "I will help you!" or "I am watching over you!".

Constant reference is made to "good spirits". Apparently there are "mocking spirits", "frivolous spirits" etc. Are there "bad spirits" which may disturb the development of treatments?

According to information provided by some experts on the subject, there are no "bad spirits"; instead there are "ignorant spirits", "spirits who do not know goodness", and "lower vibration spirits". There are also those who claim the existence of bad spirits just as there are bad people. This question involves details which the author does not know very much about. Negative influence on the part of spirits in procedures would indeed be possible, but this does not occur, according to the medium João, due to the positive energy sent by the Casa's protecting spirits and the energy gathered by the assistant mediums. Therefore, the environment at the Casa is only suitable for "good spirits".

Are spiritual healing and mediumistic manifestations new topics in the history of humankind?

No, both spiritual healing and mediumistic manifestations have been reported throughout history, as the following excerpt attests:

> Civilizations such as those which thrived in Atlantis, Lemuria, China, Hebrew land, Egypt, Persia, Caldea, Carthago, Assiria, Greece, Babylon, India, Germania or Arabia provide evidence through their history, myths or folklore that mediumistic phenomena started appearing in all corners of the globe at almost the same time and without special privileges. They were manifest in all human gatherings. Mediumistic phenomenology was even evidenced in objects and bellicose purposes of these primitive societies and influenced them greatly, even though its reality was veiled by the symbolism of legendary traditions.

> Scandinavians, especially Vikings, narrate their encounters with gods, witches, mermaids, and fascinating entities which sprung from mysterious mists and followed them during full moon nights. The Vikings' own music reveals a tone of occult inquiry or imaginative expectation, and its melodies suggest both the unorthodox and the surprising in the life of the physical man.

Histories and legends turned into musical language by Wagner in his symphonic pieces or grand operas confirm the spirit of religiosity and belief in the invisible world on the part of Germanic and Anglo-Saxon peoples. They paid tribute to gods, geniuses, and numens, and regarded them as inhabitants of a strange world that was radically different from the world of humans.[50]

Detailed information date from the 14th century BC:

Nefertiti, high priestess of the Sun, taught her disciples in the healing art, known to us nowadays as "Reiki" or spiritual passes. The priestesses were connected to medical procedures of the House of Life and healed many patients through the simple imposition of hands united with mental power and spiritual influences of the Wider World. Isis was already a remarkable magnetizer who performed fantastic cures. By using the astral essence of the sun's rays, priestesses obtained results which impressed traditional physicians graduated in Thebes or Memphis. Radical forms of treatment, such as trepanation of the skull, were unnecessary in Akhetaton. Even brain tumors were simply disintegrated through magnetic healing, which restored a patient's health entirely.[51]

In the Bible there are various references to mediumistic manifestations:

Although mediumistic events described in the Bible are veiled by the symbolism of the Hebrew race or by religious poetry, they are in fact as specific and positive as those which Allan Kardec and other Spiritist authors revealed in their studies. Due to the restricted space at our disposal in this book, we will mention only a few of the main mediumistic phenomena present in the Old and the New Testaments, all of which prove the manifestation of mediumship in those days and thus exempt the Spiritist doctrine from having invented such phenomena for doctrinary purposes.

The mediumistic phenomenon of "materialization" and "direct voice", for instance, is indisputably registered in 1 Samuel, chapter 28, verses 11, 12, and 15, when Saul, on the eve of commanding a harsh battle, decided to consult a notorious pythoness of those days with the wish of hearing the soul of Samuel, a former powerful commander of the Israeli armies who was already deceased and was buried in Ramatha, his home land. This is how the Bible reports such facts in the cited verses: "Then the woman said, "Whom shall I bring up for you?" He said, "Bring up Samuel for me.""

[50] RAMATIS. In: *Mediunidade de Cura*, p. 33 and 34.
[51] PARANHOS, Roger Bottini. *Akhenaton* – A Revolução Espiritual do Antigo Egito, p. 189/190.

When the woman saw Samuel, she cried out with a loud voice. And the woman said to Saul, "Why have you deceived me? You are Saul." Then Samuel (the materialized spirit) said to Saul, "Why have you disturbed me by bringing me up?"

In Job, chapter 4, verses 13, 15, and 16, the prophet says:

"Amid thoughts from visions of the night, when deep sleep falls on men, a spirit glided past my face; the hair of my flesh stood up. It stood still, but I could not discern its appearance. A form was before my eyes; there was silence, then I heard a voice".

In both cases the materialization of spirits and the phenomenon of "direct voice" are perfectly evidenced, and they are best translated by the sentence: "[…] then I heard a voice".

In 2 Kings, chapter 6, verses 5 and 6, the prophet Elisha produces the phenomenon of levitation which is notorious in Spiritist sessions of physical phenomena, according to the following excerpt: "But as one was felling a log, his axe head fell into the water, and he cried out, "Alas, my master! It was borrowed." Then the man of God (the prophet Elisha) said, "Where did it fall?" When he showed him the place, he cut off a stick and threw it in there and made the iron float". There is no doubt whatsoever about this fact, because in this example the act of "levitation" is proved in a spectacular way as the iron of the axe emerged on the surface of the river and out to broad daylight.

The phenomenon of materialization can be confirmed further in the following narrative from Lucas, chapter 1, verse 11: "And there appeared to Zechariah an angel of the Lord standing on the right side of the altar of incense". According to the accounts of some apostles in other biblical excerpts, an angel also materialized to the Virgin Mary and told her that she would be the mother of the Lord.

Mediumship of "transport" is perfectly implicit in the accounts of the prophet Ezekiel (chapter 3, verse 14), as follows: "The Spirit lifted me up and took me away, and I went in bitterness in the heat of my spirit, the hand of the Lord being strong upon me". Similarly, Philip (Acts, chapter 8, verses 39 and 40) explains the phenomenon thus: "And when they came up out of the water, the Spirit of the Lord carried Philip away, and the eunuch saw him no more, and went on his way rejoicing. But Philip found himself at Azotus, and as he passed through he preached the gospel to all the towns until he came to Caesarea".

Premonition was also widely performed in biblical times, for the Bible is prodigious in such prophetic reports which foresee the arrival of great beings. Malachi, chapter 4, verse 5, foresees the arrival of Elijah: ""Behold, I will send you Elijah the prophet before the great and awesome day of the Lord comes".

Isaiah was also an unusual clairvoyant. He predicted nearly a millennium in advance the arrival of Jesus and revealed details which would later serve to identify the Master's sublime character; this is illustrated in chapter 7, verses 14 and 15, of his book: "Therefore the Lord himself will give you a sign. Behold, the virgin shall conceive and bear a son, and shall call his name Immanuel (God is with us). He shall eat curds and honey when he knows how to refuse the evil and choose the good". Isaiah prophesied the birth of Jesus by a virgin, in other words, a virgin's first son can only be one who was conceived in her first marital relation. Therefore, the Master was born from a virgin, but He did not deny the Creator's unchanging physical laws or distort the peculiar genetic process of the world He inhabits. Isaiah's clairvoyance receives further proof when he indicates that Jesus would be fed with curds and honey, thus a vegetarian who would regard honey as one of His favorite foods.

It is possible to find further indisputable evidence in the Bible of the just and equitable mechanism of the Law of Karma and the processes of reincarnation, all of which are nowadays related to Spiritistic teachings. It is enough to examine the excerpt concerning the arrival of the prophet Elijah and of John the Baptist in Matthew, chapter 11, verses 13 and 14: "For all the Prophets and the Law prophesied until John, and if you are willing to accept it, he is Elijah who is to come." Another example is found in Matthew, chapter 17, verses 11 to 13: "And Jesus answered, "Elijah does come, and he will restore all things. But I tell you that Elijah has already come, and they did not recognize him [...] Then the disciples understood that he was speaking to them of John the Baptist".

Through these traditional accounts the Bible itself confirms the idea of reincarnation in those memorable times and even endorses the rectifying concept of the Law of the Karma, in which "reaping is always in tune with sowing". In 1 Kings, chapter 18, verse 40, Elijah gives the following order to his disciples: "Seize the prophets of Baal; let not one of them escape." And they seized them. And Elijah brought them down to the brook Kishon and slaughtered them there". Thus, Elijah had them slaughtered at the Kishon brook and was guilty in the face of the Law of the Karma by the kind of barbaric death which he inflicted on the priests of Baal, and which made him viable for a similar fate in future. In fact, it is the Bible itself that provides evidence of the rescue of Elijah's Karmic debt when, after having reborn on Earth in the body of the prophet John the Baptist, he was also beheaded during Herod's rule at Salome's command. The Law of the Karma was fulfilled in its merciless redeeming justice as Elijah, the former decapitator, also suffers an identical Karmic proof after having reincarnated as John the Baptist, according to the law that "he who lives by the sword, shall die by the sword", even though he was the precursor of the Messiah Himself.[52]

Mediumship plays an expressive part in the history of Brazil:

In fact, Brazil is also rich in myths and supernatural stories whose origins can be traced back to the Brazilians' fairly developed mediumistic faculty. In general they are prodigiously intuitive from a very early age. Long before Spiritist codification the natives of American lands already performed several rites which enabled them to establish a mediumistic exchange with the invisible world and thus contact disincarnated tribe companions. They also performed healing mediumship by prescribing chosen herbs or banishing evil spirits through the magical process of collective exorcisms. American natives predicted weather variations as well as the most favorable time of year for plantation and harvest, perceived signs from the occult world, and sensed epidemic or unsuitable places for their existence. The most experienced shamans foresaw the death of tribe chiefs, the birth of good warriors or the bellicose march of rival tribes, and successfully predicted the outcome of bloody disputes.

Brazilian myths are rich in mediumistic references. In the landscape of moon-lit woods the "boitatá" (a fire-snake) appears, shooting fire from its nostrils; the phantasmagoric "saci-pererê" (a one-legged black boy) appears in dark crossroads by hopping on one foot and shooting fire from his flaming eyes; in the endless prairie the headless mule runs wild; or in the shadows of misty nights, more credulous individuals claim they hear the sad moans of the "negrinho do pastoreio" (black boy from the pastoral lands).

Even though such folkloric narratives are based on myth and fantasy, they are marked by unmistakable mediumistic phenomena which provide proof of immortal life.[53]

---

[52] RAMATIS. In: *Mediunidade de Cura*, p. 40-43.
[53] RAMATIS. In: *Mediunidade de Cura*, p. 34 and 35.

5. Eliminated disease and paralyzed disease

How can one account for the fact that a given illness may be eliminated in many cases but in others a progressive illness is only paralyzed?

The author is not able to explain this.

Is it possible to know the criteria adopted when the Entity tells an attended person to seek a doctor?

No. If there are such criteria only the Entity knows. It seems that a person with a reasonable economic situation is instructed to see a doctor whenever the health problem is not too complex and may be solved by Medicine professionals.

6. Individual and group surgeries

What are individual and group surgeries like?

No member of staff at the Casa, not even the medium João, knows in advance whether a person will be submitted to individual or group surgery. It is the Entity who decides.

During attendance to the queues the Entity tells an individual to return in the afternoon, on the following day or on the following week in order to undergo surgery (group surgery). On other occasions the Entity decides to operate on a person at the moment of attendance. In this case the surgery – regardless of the infirmity – nearly always consists in eye scraping or the insertion of a Kelly clamp[54] in one of the nostrils, without anesthesia and asepsis, with a cotton bud soaked in fluidified water on its edge.

During spiritual surgery, is there any contact between João-in-Entity with the person submitted to surgery?

Not in the great majority of cases. The surgery may occur without João-in-Entity having to touch the person being submitted to it.

How does this occur?

The surgery is invisible. The author was once shown by the Entity a scar being formed on a person who had undergone surgery but who had not been touched by João-in-Entity.

---

[54] This instrument is a kind of sharp edged tweezers with a handle, similar to scissors.

What happens if someone is designated for surgery and does not turn up?

There will be no consequences apart from the fact that the person will not receive spiritual aid.

Are there any statistics concerning spiritual cures recorded by Casa de Dom Inácio?

No, the Casa is not concerned with any kind of records. However, the following table reveals results of interviews with Casa visitors as part of a post-graduate research study[55]:

a) Patients who received cures
yes 74,40%
no 24,00%
did not answer..............01,60%

b) Type of cure
physical 39,20%
spiritual........................36,00%
did not receive cure 24,80%

c) Currently receiving medical treatment?
yes 43,20%
no 56,80%

d) Do you know people who benefited from spiritual healing?
yes 93,20%
no...................................06,80%

e) Is faith important in order to obtain spiritual healing?
yes 93,80%
no 06,20%

f) To whom was spritual healing attributed?
medium........................05,40%
espirito 08,00%
faith..............................64,40%
Casa de Dom Inácio 04,00%
mental capacityl............01,20%
all of the above 17,00%

g) Do you believe in the existence of a spirit together with the medium in the healing process:
yes 95,80%
no 02,60%
in doubt........................01,60%

---

[55] SAVARIS, Alfredina Arlete. *Curas Paranormais Realizadas por João Teixeira de Faria*, p. 87.

What is the highest percentage of illnesses which afflict Casa visitors?

There are no records or even a concern in recording such details. Body illnesses are several but there are also spiritual illnesses. Nevertheless, despite the lack of concern for statistics, the author's observations seem to point to cancer in its various forms.

7. Spiritual healing involving cuts

Did the surgeries witnessed by the author involve cuts?

They seldom did, most surgeries consisted only of a prayer. Other individual operations consisted only of passing hands over the area of infirmity. Such hand contact did not occur in several other cases. Strictly speaking, surgeries involved eye scraping and deep cleaning of the nasal cavity.

Are surgeries with cuts necessary?

The author does not think so. In the past such procedures were quite common. As a recommendation of Casa lawyers due to criminal lawsuits filed against the medium João, these surgeries are not performed.

If surgeries involving cuts are not necessary, why are they performed, albeit sporadically?

As previously stated they are rare, and when they are performed the Entity knows what it is doing. Normally such procedures are carried out when a person only believes in healing by cuts, when a non-believing doctor goes to the Casa, when journalists and researchers wish to see a surgery of this kind etc. However, surgeries with cuts for the sole purpose of public showing are not performed.

When surgery involves physical contact other than by hands, what instruments are used?

The most commonly used instruments are a small kitchen knife for scraping of the ocular globe and a Kelly clamp with cotton soaked in fluidified water which is inserted into the nasal cavity.

Has the author witnessed surgeries with cuts?

Yes, several. The rare surgeries of this kind were quite rustic procedures and employed scalpels and needles for sutures, without anesthesia or asepsis. There was virtually no bleeding.

Of all the surgeries witnessed by the author, did any attract his attention in particular?

Yes, several. It touches any person's sensitivity to witness, for instance, the cutting of a person's scalp and, without opening the braincase, the "squeezing" of the cut's edges (with ungloved fingers) in order to remove a brain tumor. This procedure lasted only a few minutes and the medium João-in-Entity did not even glance at the surgical area.

What would be expected to exist but in reality does not in spiritual healing?

There is no anesthesia, asepsis, blood in normal amounts (when cuts are made), pre-surgery measures nor pain.

Does one ever feel pain in healing?

As the author was told, an individual who is being submitted to spiritual surgery may feel some pain if he/she is not sufficiently concentrated, if there is lack of concentration on the part of assistant mediums, if arms, legs, and hands are crossed, and if there is too much talking or noise made by people awaiting attendance in the assembly room.

What could possibly occur but in fact does not?

Hypnosis, loss of conscience, acupuncture, lethargy technique, bleeding, and infections.

8. Number of surgery patients

How many people are spiritually operated on at the same time?
As many as the Entity wishes.

Is there a limit as to the number of group surgeries performed in one day?

If there is, only the Entity knows it. The Casa has no records in this regard and no concerns over it. The author, out of curiosity, attempted to count on a few occasions. In Abadiânia it is quite normal for 100 to 200 surgeries to be performed a day. Outside Abadiânia the number ranges from 150 to 300. In Germany, in only one period (afternoon), the author counted 278 people in a collective surgery.

How many people are seen in one day by the medium João-in-Entity at the Casa or elsewhere?

There is no concern over registering the exact number of services. At the Casa the attendance of 500 to 1000 people a day is normal, but if more visitors arrive, they will all be attended. When services are performed outside Abadiânia, in Brazil or in other countries, the number increases and may be over 2000 people a day.

What changes in attendance when the number of visitors is greater?

Queues flow at a faster pace and procedures finish later than usual. Apart from these factors all else remains the same.

9. Duration of surgeries

What is the duration of group surgeries?

Group surgeries last on average 2 minutes, regardless of the number of people, be it 30, 50, 60, 80 or over 100.

If a person is individually submitted to spiritual surgery, does this surgery also last at least 2 minutes?

Normally they do, but there are cases in which an individual surgery may last five, ten, fifteen or more minutes.

Would not group surgeries logically demand more time?

There is not only a spirit who performs collective surgeries, but a team which may be made up of hundreds or thousands of good spirits.

How long does a treatment of spiritual healing last?

It varies depending on the case. The author knows of a real case in which the treatment consisted of a single group surgery which lasted about 2 minutes. He also knows a person whose treatment lasted for more than twelve years. Spiritual healing was accomplished in both cases.

10. Review and discharge

What is a review?

A review consists in the assessment by the Entity on whether a regular surgery recovery occurred.

What is discharge?

It means that everything went well and that the person is cured. This person will only return to the Casa for leisure or for some other reason.

When an illness is internal - therefore making a visible outcome impossible - how does the benefited person know if he/she is cured?

Once the Entity gives discharge during review and tells him/her that, if they so wish, they may take the necessary exams in order to verify the non-existence of the illness.

11. Rest and post-surgery

Are all surgery patients transported to the ward for rest?

Not all of them. There is no transport or rest in the ward as far as group surgeries are concerned. In individual surgeries, the Entity occasionally authorizes a person to leave by walking naturally.

What is the purpose of the Entity in placing a person submitted to surgery in repose?

It seems that people who are submitted to surgery are a little dizzy from spiritual anesthesia, therefore rest is recommended. Apart from that, it is necessary to recover one's energies especially due to the natural emotional tension.

How are patients subsequently monitored, be the surgery individual or collective?

Patients are not monitored.

Are not patients even monitored in order to verify whether infection occurred?

No. There are only post-surgery recommendations for both individuals and groups. However, infection does not occur.

What immediately follows spiritual surgery?

In the case of an individual surgery, an individual is usually taken to the ward and remains there resting for at least one hour before being discharged. In the case of collective surgeries, the patient is discharged and walks out normally.

Does the patient receive some kind of orientation regarding post-surgery?

Yes, general guidelines are transmitted to those submitted to individual surgeries by the person in charge of the ward or to surgery groups by a Casa assistant. Orientation is given in English for those who do not understand Portuguese.

What kind of orientation is provided?

Mainly orientation regarding rest and nourishment.

Is there no recommendation of a return for review?

Yes, depending on the case.

Is there any scientific explanation for the non-existence of problems after spiritual surgeries?

The author does not have enough information in this regard.

Are there any grave consequences for those submitted to spiritual surgery who do not follow post-surgery recommendations?

The only consequence is that they will not receive the benefit of the intended cure. People use their free will to decide whether to follow recommendations or not.

A person's conduct is important before, during, and after surgery. Before surgery a person must be spiritually prepared for it; during the surgery, a person must direct all thoughts to God; and after surgery, a person must follow recommendations regarding rest (saving of energies) and nourishment.

12. Recurrence

Is recurrence (return of a health problem) possible in the case of spiritual surgeries?

Yes, it is.

Why may recurrence occur?

For several reasons: if one does not follow the diet, does not rest or does not merit healing.

13. Medication

For which illnesses is the Passiflora medication prescribed?

For several illnesses. In fact, Passiflora is the only medication that is prescribed and sold.

What happens if a prescription is given and a person does not wish to take the medication?

Everyone is free to take the medication or not.

How is it possible for a single medication to be used in the treatment of different people and illnesses?

As previously explained by the medium João (chapter II, n. 5), Passiflora capsules are energized by spirits in specific ways that suit each person.

If one excludes spiritual effects and considers solely physical effects, may Passiflora be regarded as an innocuous medication?

As for the physical aspect, it may. Passion fruit powder is nothing more than a tranquilizer, an equivalent to herbal tea. The medication may in fact be innocuous to the body but it always produces benefits for the spirit.

Therefore, to a certain extent, this question relates to the so-called "placebo effect"[56]: the medication is innocuous, but will it produce effects if a person believes in it?

Yes, in some way.

Is any medication used during surgeries, even without anesthesia and asepsis?

No, only cotton soaked in fluidified water.

Is it possible to obtain a cure only by taking Passiflora?

Yes, just as a cure will be possible only by drinking fluidified water or even by not taking any kind of medication in the case of a person who has faith and merits healing.

---

[56] Placebo: neutral substance devoid of pharmacological effects which is occasionally prescribed in order to make a patient relieve symptoms by the simple act of believing in the medication's therapeutic properties. In: *Revista Parapsicologia*, year 2, n. 23, p. 38.

Is there any contraindication in taking Passiflora together with medication prescribed by doctors?

No.

Is there any explanation for prescribing medication to a person who does not merit spiritual healing?

Based on the author's scarce knowledge on the subject and on explanations provided by older Casa visitors, energized medication aims to make a person fit to reach merit. Whenever one takes the medication he/she will have their thoughts turned to Casa de Dom Inácio, which indicates "good thoughts".

Is there any recommendation regarding the suspension of medication prescribed by doctors?

Absolutely not, as has previously been stated (chapter I, n. 4).

In case of healing of the cause, will the effect in the body disappear?

Yes. The existing literature states that healing takes place in the perispirit which is where the cause is located. The physical problem which affects the body is a consequence, and as spiritual surgery attacks the cause, the effect will disappear.

14. Curious references

Is the word "cancer" – which for some reason causes strong impact – normally uttered?

No illness attracts great attention at the Casa, but it is worth mentioning that the author often heard the Entity say that a person's problem consisted (in the past) of a "spider"[57]. The author did not know what this word meant at first, but was later told by an older visitor that it was a reference to "cancer".

Is the author aware of other curious references?

Yes. He does not know if it was the same Entity who occasionally used the expression "white coat" in reference to "doctors" without any pejorative connotation.

---

[57] The author does not know whether this expression is used by only one Entity.

What is the reason for the expression "white coat"?

In the author's opinion this reference is motivated by the fact that many doctors use a white jacket while working.

What is the meaning of the expression "carry it away" used by the Entity at the end of an individual spiritual surgery?

It should be understood as "take it away". It means that a person was operated on and needs to rest for at least one hour in the ward in order to recover fully.

Despite the expression "carry it away", Casa assistants use a wheelchair to transport people.

What are such chairs for surgery patients like?

They are rustic wheelchairs with the sole purpose of transporting surgery patients from the Entity room to the ward.

15. Illness and impossibility of pregnancy

What is the definition of "illness"?

There is a medical definition and a spiritual definition. In general and imprecise terms, the former defines 'illness' as a biological alteration of a health condition. Health, in its turn, is a state of good physical and psychic disposition translated in the perfect functioning of the body.

The latter defines 'illness' as the consequence of "the maladjustment of the magnetic potentiality of bodily complex"[58].

Is impossibility of pregnancy an illness?

Depending on the case it may be a physical problem of irregular functioning or a spiritual problem.

Which is prone to illness, the body or the spirit?

The spirit. The body is only a material exterior. The cause lies in the spirit but the effect is shown in the body.

---

[58] CAPELLI, Esse. *Mediunidade* – Elucidações Práticas, p. 93.

What causes an illness?

There are various causes. Every negative thought and conduct may produce illnesses. In addition, the notorious "deadly sins" may also result in body illnesses: wrath, lust, gluttony, sloth, pride, greed, and envy.

In what way may spiritual treatment help a woman - considered sterile by conventional medicine - to get pregnant?

According to the author's scarce knowledge on the subject there is no scientific explanation, just as there is no explanation regarding the cure of certain illnesses which are considered irreversible.

16. Desperate and terminal patients

Is this book able to kindle the hope of desperate people with serious health or existential problems of finding a solution for their afflictions?

They may have hope but they should not think that they have found the solution. This book is only an account of what goes on at Casa de Dom Inácio. Spiritual healing does exist: all may seek it but its achievement depends on each person's merit. The search may occur in any religion or temple; a person may not deserve healing or a certain health problem may constitute "karma". It is worth trying, whatever the situation.

What does 'karma' mean?[59]

In terms of an explanation for non-specialists, 'karma' is the negative balance of a spirit's past conduct, whereas merit is the positive balance.

Is it possible to attenuate karma?

Yes, through good deeds. Human beings are free to perform all kinds of deeds, good or evil. Without free will humans would be nothing more than machines.

Is a visit to Casa de Dom Inácio valid even for a terminal patient who has given up hope of cure by conventional medicine?

No, terminal patients may aggravate their health during the trip. In addition, reports of deaths during trips result in juridical problems for the medium João.

---

[59] "Karma is the debt or credit in the face of Divine Justice, a result of our actions in previous incarnations". In: *Revista Espírita Allan Kardec*, ano XIII, n. 53, Goiânia, julho de 2005, p. 6.

There was once an episode concerning a foreigner in terminal state who had suffered from AIDS for over fifteen years and had abandoned all kinds of medical treatment for two years. He traveled to Casa de Dom Inácio in search of spiritual comfort but passed away in Abadiânia. As a result the medium João was accused of homicide and this episode was widely divulged by the press.

How may terminal patients be prevented from seeking Casa de Dom Inácio?

Tour guides are instructed not to take terminal patients to Abadiânia, but nothing can be done to prevent someone from traveling on their own.

If an illness has reached an advanced stage is spiritual healing impossible?

It may or may not be, depending on the case. It is widely known that the sooner one seeks medical help for a given health problem, the greater possibility of a successful treatment. The same applies to spiritual healing: spiritual treatment must be sought as soon as possible. Preventive treatment is also recommended, as is the case in conventional medicine.

What measures may be adopted by Casa de Dom Inácio for a terminal patient who seeks some sort of spiritual aid?

It is recommended that a friend of the patient takes a photograph or a personal object and hands it over to the Entity. It is an alternative of long-distance treatment in which the Entity prescribes a suitable medication for a given infirmity.

17. Attendance outside Abadiânia

Does the medium João offer services in other locations outside Casa de Dom Inácio in Abadiânia?

Yes, he attends people in other cities, states, and even in other countries.

When the medium João offers services outside Abadiânia, whether in Brazil or abroad, how are assistant mediums selected?

This task is a responsibility of the attendance organizers. There are mediums in every locality. In addition, as queues are attended, the Entity invites people who possess mediumship to "sit in the current", which means to offer energetic help to the effective proceeding of works. Whenever the current is weak due to deficiency of assistant mediums – in qualitative and not quantitative terms – the "current" is "held" by the medium João. On these occasions he spends a great amount of energy and thus needs prolonged rest in order to recover his strength at the end of attendance.

Is it possible for the current to be so weak as to disturb spiritual attendance?

It has never happened before. As previously stated, if the current is weak the medium João spends more energy and later requires a longer period of rest after attendance.

Is spiritual attendance outside Abadiânia complete?

Generally yes. However, in certain situations, the Entity may tell a person who has been attended to go to Abadiânia.

What happens if a person cannot afford travel and accommodation expenses?

The Entity knows if a person is able to afford expenses or not. During attendance outside Abadiânia the author once heard the Entity state that a person who had been attended could not afford to go to Abadiânia. For that reason the person could undergo spiritual surgery at that very moment.

Procedures in Abadiânia are offered for free. What happens in other locations?

In Brazil procedures are always free of charge. In foreign countries that depends on the organizers. Travel, accommodation, and food expenses of the medium João and his team are considerable, in addition to other expenses. Normally organizers charge fees from participants in order to cover such expenses. Profit is not prohibited but the commercial aspect should never be the main objective of attendance.

Are there norms for attendance abroad?

Yes, there are general norms, but the medium João has the last word. What is known is that attendance abroad is only performed after spiritual authorization has been given.

18. Real stories of spiritual cures

Which criteria were adopted for registration and publication of forty real stories regarding spiritual cures?

Initially it was necessary to document a high number of people who benefited from treatments that included physical and spiritual illnesses. Afterwards the author considered the idea of presenting cures based on several illnesses: cancer, degenerative illnesses, hepatitis, leukemia, diabetes, palpitations, Parkinson's disease, Alzheimer's disease, angina, syphilis, paralysis, allergy, pneumonia, existential problems, and other unknown illnesses. However, listing the names of illnesses involved knowledge of medical technical terms which the author does not possess and he might have thus incurred in error. Once this strategy was discarded, the author considered presenting illnesses by their localization in the body: face, eyes, mouth, neck, spinal column, heart, liver, spleen, throat, lung, stomach, kidneys, skin, blood, prostate, arms, legs etc. The author even attempted to consider factors such as nationality (Brazilian or foreign), sex, cultural background, among others. The initial target was 100 real cases to be selected and published.

On one occasion the Entity told the author not to worry about an elevated number of registers and that a sample ranging from twenty to forty people who benefited from spiritual cures would be sufficient. From that moment on the author decided on forty selected people. He abandoned the idea of sampling by sex, nationality, age, marital status, names of diseases, parts of the body, level of formal education etc, and instead simply listed concrete cases and put the names of the benefited people in alphabetical order.[60]

Which criteria were used to exclude from the list people who obtained spiritual cures?

Even after having at his disposal individual accounts of people who benefited from spiritual cures, the author excluded the following cases:

   a) Doctors: in order to preserve countless doctors who attend Casa de Dom Inácio and/or obtained spiritual cures and in order to prevent them from being questioned by respective Medicine Regional Councils due to alleged ethical violations;

---

[60] Only the last two cases are not listed in alphabetical order.

b) Artists, politicians, and authorities: public exposure of their names might result in serious embarrassment;

c) Children: they are in no condition to make statements. The stories hereby included followed the Entity's recommendation and also reveal statements by parents;

d) Cases of pregnancy in women considered sterile by conventional medicine: such exposure might bring future embarrassment for the child;

e) Long-distance cures: there was no personal contact or actual attendance at Casa de Dom Inácio;

f) Cases of obsessions: possible embarrassment for those benefited was taken into consideration;

g) Aids victims: the author followed a recommendation given by the Entity itself, as the simple fact of people admitting they had the disease and were healed would be enough to drive others away. It must be stated that several healed people offered to make statements and consented to the inclusion of their names in this book;

h) All those who had any kind of doubts over authorizing their names for publication.

Why did not the author prefer to select people with a higher cultural level in order to avoid remarks - which are somewhat true - that less instructed people are more easily influenced?

All people are equal. Illnesses do not choose sex, age, nationality, color, social status or cultural background. All forms of discrimination are odious.

Did the selection of real cases prove difficult?

Difficulties were natural considering the great number of interviewed people.

How many people who benefited from spiritual healing were interviewed?

Approximately 300 people, in addition to those who gave statements in registry offices and those who wrote letters expressing obtained results.

Were all the people hereby presented with their true stories really cured?

Each person is responsible for his/her account, so it is up to the reader to arrive at personal conclusions without any interference from others. Nevertheless recurrence may indeed occur or a new infirmity may appear.

Is it possible to reveal a person's name, the spiritual treatment he/she received, and the obtained cure without this person's consent?

The Brazilian law states that a citizen's privacy and image must be respected[61]. It is not possible to make public someone's identity and cure without his/her prior authorization. Therefore, in addition to verbal agreement, a written authorization was also obtained. Each selected person filled in a statement or presented it by a public instrument at a registry office. This statement reveals personal identification, health problem, performed treatment, obtained result, and the date on which this information was given.

Some people wrote to the Casa spontaneously and reported their cures. Once the author got in contact with them they authorized the publication of such cures. When necessary, interpreters were used for verbal explanations and translators for written information.

Which real cases of spiritual cures may be mentioned?

The following cases are examples of spiritual cures. It is once again stated that the author attempted to record the words used by interviewees as faithfully as possible, regardless of whether the technical terminology used was correct or not.

It is also necessary to state that the health problems and addresses of benefited people refer to information presented on the dates the statements were made. Therefore, changes may have occurred since then.

| ÂNGELA MONNERAT HABERFELD

Brazilian, married, systems analyst, ID n. 1.734.825 – IFP/RJ, CPF* n. 465.939.187-68, lives at SGAN 914, Módulo H, Bloco D, Apto. 234, Brasília (DF).

Health problems – Cancer of the ovary. I underwent surgery a long time ago. The gynecologist extracted the cancerous tissue from my gynecological organs and left part of it which should be removed by a proctologist because it was located considerably below the abdomen. I was submitted

---

[61] CF, art. 5. X: "intimacy, private life, honor, and the image of people are inviolable, and the right for compensation for material or moral damage caused by such violation is assured".

* CPF stands for 'Cadastro de Pessoa Física' (Physical Person Registration) – T.N.

to a tomography before starting chemotherapy – six sessions in all. The doctor suggested chemotherapy in an attempt to reduce or eliminate the cancer and to facilitate a second surgery or even make it unnecessary.

Performed treatment – I was told of the existence of Casa de Dom Inácio by a friend. I went to Abadiânia and the Entity only prescribed Passiflora (four bottles). Forty days later I returned to the Casa and received more medication. After forty days I was submitted to an ultrasound scan at the end of chemotherapy which revealed the permanence of the mass from the previous surgery. I returned to Casa de Dom Inácio. The Entity told me I was well and prescribed four more bottles of Passiflora. I took the medication and after the next surgery the proctologist concluded that the "mass" which appeared in the tomography did not exist. The doctor could not understand how the tissue was visible in the tomography but nothing was found in the area which could be surgically removed. Afterwards he called on other doctors to verify the unexplainable. When I returned to Casa de Dom Inácio the Entity declared me healed.

Result – I have recently been submitted to exams and no cancer was verified. I am healed and I still return to the Casa moved by gratitude, by a pleasant feeling of being there, and in order to take friends with health problems.

|ANGELIM DA COSTA FARIA

Brazilian, married, trader, born February 25, 1966, ID n. 358.404 – SSP/MT, CIC* n. 415.696.361-68, lives at Rua Arinos, n. 894, Centro, Colíder (MT).

Health problems – Years ago I felt the beginning of the illness. It started when my vision began to darken, which led me to seek an ophthalmologist in Sinop (MT). The latter instructed me to see a neurologist at the town of Cáceres (MT) who had previously performed a surgery by placing a

---

* CIC stands for Cartão de Identificação do Contribuinte (Taxpayer Identification Card) – T.N.

right ventricular derivative valve. In view of the suspicion that my problem was somehow related to the valve, the neurologist referred me to the city of Cuiabá (MT) so I could undergo a computerized tomography of the brain. No abnormalities were verified. When I returned to Cáceres and showed the tomography result to my doctor he told me to remain in observation for fifteen days because my vision was still darkened. However, no abnormalities were verified. Afterwards he instructed me to return to the ophthalmologist and do another exam. Before I did this exam I felt a strong headache and entered into superficial coma, and was taken to Cuiabá for internment. New exams did not reveal anything unusual. As my health condition was critical, the doctor – unsure of what was the exact problem - wanted a new surgery in order to change the valve. The doctor who had placed the valve warned my family against a new surgery. The previous doctor said that nothing could be done and suggested a more advanced medical treatment in São Paulo. After being unable to find a vacancy in São Paulo I went to Vitória (ES), where some relatives of mine live. I was submitted to another computerized tomography of the brain and this time doctors observed signs of cerebral atrophy. I did not show any improvement under medical care and therefore returned to Colíder, the town I lived in. After three months, at the brink of death, I began to vomit and was taken by relatives to Cuiabá. I was submitted to another computerized tomography and nothing was observed.

Performed treatment – One day my wife heard from an uncle who resided in Vitória of a certain healer who lived in the town of Abadiânia. She went to Casa de Dom Inácio and took only a picture of me. She remained in Abadiânia for two weeks due to recommendation by the Entity Dr. Augusto. As soon as she returned home and appeared at the bedroom door, she felt that something miraculous had happened because I looked at her and smiled, and she ran and hugged me. I was also able to hug her back. After this visible improvement in my condition my wife returned to Casa de Dom Inácio five times in intervals of thirty days, and every time she returned home I was better. At the sixth visit I was able to accompany her and we went by bus. I returned to Casa de Dom Inácio on other occasions on my own.

Result – Ever since my wife's first visit to Casa de Dom Inácio I did not seek any more doctors. I did not feel ill anymore and I enjoy perfect health. I am healthy, I weigh 76 kg, I often walk and ride a bike and I follow the recommendation of the Entity Dr. Augusto.

⌊Antônio Fernandes Galvão

Brazilian, federal public worker, retired, born November 9, 1941, ID n. 1657235468363-SSP/SP, CPF n. 010.345.961-87, lives at Rua GB-36, Qd. 60, Lt. 21-A, Jardim Guanabara III, Goiânia (GO).

Health problems – For several years I suffered from left facial paralysis. When I woke up one morning to brush my teeth I felt that the left side of my face and my mouth were crooked and trembling; I was not even able to move the ocular globe or the left eyelid. As a result I went to the Health Center in Monte Alegre (GO) and was examined by a doctor who instructed me to go to Goiânia (GO) for a more careful examination. In spite of her suggestion I decided to go to Campos Belos (GO) which is a relatively big town about 35 km from Monte Alegre and therefore has a hospital and a health clinic. I was submitted to an electrocardiogram which revealed that there was a blockage in the veins that accessed the heart. Some medications were prescribed, I remained in town for observation (in case of any emergency), and afterwards I was told that I would need to start physiotherapy because my face was deformed. I remained in town for a few days but my condition worsened every day.

Performed treatment – As I had once been cured of a terrible headache at Casa de Dom Inácio years before, I decided to go to Abadiânia. In the first consultation the Entity Dr. Augusto told me I needed to undergo surgery. On the same day, during the afternoon, I was submitted to invisible surgery and three bottles of tablets were prescribed.

Result – I felt better right after the surgery and returned to the hotel where I was staying. As soon as I got there I realized that my left eye was winking and my face was getting normal again. I sought neurologists and cardiologists and did echocardiography, blood, and Holter exams. When the neurologist failed to see anything abnormal in the exams, he concluded that I was completely cured and there would be no need for me to be submitted to electroencephalogram or to an x-ray of the head.

| ANTÔNIO FERNANDO DE SOUZA CALMON FILHO

Brazilian, married, trader, born April 26, 1969, ID n. 2903494-SSP/PE, CPF n. 611.825.164-91, lives at Rua Aristarco Lopes, n. 900, Apt. 403, Petrolina (PE).

Health problems – I am the father of Maria Fernanda Barros e Silva Calmon, born March 19, 2000, as registered in the Birth Certificate provided by the Civil Registry Office of Natural Persons of the Subdistrict of Vitória, Comarca* of Salvador (BA), book A-393, page 78, Term 137077. She had a deterioration of the first vertebra (C-1) whose cause could not be diagnosed by conventional medicine. This illness prevented her from moving her neck and even from walking due a gradual loss of balance. Doctors revealed that a C-1 lesion was incompatible with her life and could not be cured. They also informed that they did not know of any case of cure in medical literature and, if they witnessed such a case, they would publish it in a specialized journal of Medicine. Since the beginning of the problem until the identification of the lesion the illness was diagnosed by doctors as mere stiff neck. The fourteenth doctor was the one who identified the C-1 vertebra lesion even though he was not able to state the cause. It must be said that this illness appeared when my daughter was one year and ten months old and perfectly healthy. However, she woke up one day and was unable to move her neck.

---

* Territorial division of the judicial system in Brazil – T.N.

Performed treatment – My daughter was submitted only once to a spiritual surgery performed by the Entity Dr. Augusto de Almeida and continued the treatment for some time.

Result – At the age of 2 years and 6 months, after treatment at Casa de Dom Inácio, my daughter had already recovered completely, according to findings emitted by Santa Catarina Hospital, located at Av. Paulista, n. 200, São Paulo (SP).

⌊ARTHUR HENRIQUE RIOS DOS SANTOS

Brazilian, divorced, stonemason, lives at Rua Castelo Branco, n. 2.280, Apt. 104, Vila Velha (ES).

Health problems – Years ago I suffered a work accident when I worked as a stonemason in Sydney, New South Wales, Australia. A block of eighty tied bricks weighing 120 kg fell on my left leg and crushed nerves and ligaments. Graft and drain were placed in my leg. From then on my life changed completely. I was submitted to six surgeries in Australia, a first world country, but to no use. I felt terrible pain and swelling. On one occasion I was submitted to an application of needles on the lombar region in order to relieve the pain. The pain did not lessen, so two more surgeries were set. I used a walking stick and an ankle support to reduce the pain caused by ankle movements, which prevented me from wearing shoes and sandals.

Performed treatment – As soon as I found out about Casa de Dom Inácio I traveled to Abadiânia. In the first consultation my ankle was examined, some medications were prescribed, and I was given the recommendation of returning there five times. One night at home, while I slept – I was already taking medication –, I was invisibly operated on in my dream by a female Entity who I thought was Sister Scheilla. The spirit kept telling me not to worry, because I felt a lot of pain and often cried. During my second visit to Casa de Dom Inácio I was again submitted to an invisible surgery and the Entity took the walking stick from me. I returned on three other occasions following recommendations.

Result – I was completely healed and later began to walk 14 km every day without feeling anything abnormal.

⎰BENNO HORST

Brazilian, married, retired, born October 17, 1924, ID n. 1070188709-SSP/RS, CPF n. 122.203.610-04, lives at Rua 03 de Outubro, n. 47, Bairro Languiru, Teotônia (RS).

Health problems – Some years ago a tiny lump appeared on the left side of my face in the jaw area. The lump did not hurt, but it grew rapidly and deformed my face. It was diagnosed as a malignant tumor.

Performed treatment – I sought Casa de Dom Inácio several times and used the prescribed medication appropriately. On one of the visits the Entity told me to seek a doctor in my home town for I would be cured. I was then submitted to two surgeries in Teotônia, my home town: the first aimed to extract the malignant lump and the second involved plastic surgery. I did not feel pain in either of the surgeries.

Result – I returned to Casa de Dom Inácio on a few occasions only to express thanks and gratitude, because I am now completely cured.

⎰BIANCA PAOLA CASSEL

Brazilian, single, student, born June 7, 1980, lives at Rua XV de Novembro, n. 3164, Santo Ângelo (RS).

Health problems – At the age of two I lost my vision, and this lasted until the age of four. As soon as my loss of vision was detected I was taken to Belo Horizonte, Minas Gerais, and admitted to the ophthalmologic clinic of the Ilton Rocha Institute, but I did not obtain positive results there.

Performed treatment – When I was four years old I was referred to Casa de Dom Inácio. On my second day at the Casa I began to see, and the treatment lasted until 2000.

Result – Since the second day of treatment at Casa de Dom Inácio until the day on which this statement was written, my vision returned.

Observation: The child was supervised by her mother because of her age.

CARLOS ALBERTO DA SILVA BANHO

Brazilian, married, retired, ID n. M-463.932, SSP/MG, CPF n. 090.567.426-04, lives at SQN 314, Bl. F, Apto. 110, Brasília (DF).

Health problems – After being submitted to specific exams doctors discovered that I had hepatitis C. Once the biopsy was performed the result was "Active chronic lobular hepatitis". Medical recommendation consisted of two options: to be submitted to the only known treatment for hepatitis C based on an expensive drug called Interferon, whose side effects are almost unbearable and whose percentage of cure ranges only from 30 to 40%; or to live with the disease in the hope of its slow evolution and that an effective drug might be produced. Once the treatment with Interferon began I could not bear the drug's side effects so I abandoned the treatment after a few months.

Performed treatment – At my mother's request, who had already been healed of a problem in her column, I sought Casa de Dom Inácio. I was submitted to a long treatment, I took the prescribed medicines, and I followed the diet prescribed by the Entity. Two years later the exams already indicated rates below reference. I continued with the spiritual treatment.

Result – The laboratory exams solicited by the Entity revealed rates below reference. The upper abdominal ultrasound scan which was performed by a specialist revealed the following diagnostic: "homogeneous liver, normal volume, normoechogenic parenchyma shows only slight periportal hyperechogenicity. Supra-hepatic veins and the portal system (measuring 11,9 mm) have normal calibers. There is no evidence of dilation of infra or extra-hepatic biliary veins". Conclusion: echographic study without evidence of abnormalities.

DOUM BOUYA FODE

Swiss, married, UN worker, Passport n. 9205973, born September 24, 1953, lives at 16 ch, de Tremessaz 1222, Vesenaz, Geneva, Switzerland.

Health problems – Pneumonia which started in Africa in 1968. I was sent to Switzerland and I took medications for 25 years which did not produce any results.

Performed treatment – One day I saw something on TV about Abadiânia. Therefore I decided to try this alternative and got on the first flight. I traveled to Casa de Dom Inácio, saw João, took Passiflora, and was submitted to two surgeries in two weeks.

Result – After taking the medication I went to the doctor. An x-ray was taken and it revealed that my lung had improved miraculously. The new x-ray was contrasted with the old one and doctors could not understand how that had happened. They asked me what I had done. I told them that if they believed in God they should follow me to Abadiânia. I am now cured of pneumonia. I am very happy with the medium João, the Entities, and all the volunteers at Casa de Dom Inácio. Thank you very much!

DERALDO MENGERN DE CASSER

Brazilian, single, stonemason, ID n. 8038006246-SSP/RS, CIC n. 626.617.950-49, lives at Rua Farol, esq. c/ Av. Leme, 664, Osório (RS).

Health problems – My illness started to appear when I suffered a fall and I hit my left leg on the ground. From that day on I began to suffer from horrible pains. I sought medical treatment, several exams were performed, but nothing was diagnosed. The pain continued and the condition evolved to what was later diagnosed as osteomyelitis. My leg revealed accentuated necrosis and doctors advised on its amputation as my only chance for survival.

Performed treatment – I became familiar with Casa de Dom Inácio through a few acquaintances, so I decided to seek it and begin spiritual treatment. I remained in Abadiânia during four days. Then I returned home and continued the treatment. As was recommended, I returned to Casa de Dom Inácio for review.

Result – As soon as the treatment began I felt considerable improvement in my leg, so I went back to work on the following week and felt only a minor pain. After review I was discharged from the treatment and I was free to return to a normal life, without feeling any more pain.

⌊ELIZABETH BARBOSA

Brazilian, tourist guide, divorced, born June 5, 1954, lives at Admiralengracht, 83II, 1057ER, Amsterdam, The Netherlands.

Health problems – Strictly speaking I did not have any physical health problems. Problems were more psychological than physical. I felt great anguish and a need to seek happiness in the outer world towards my inner self.

Performed treatment – I am Brazilian and I have lived in The Netherlands for many years. When I heard of the medium João's trip to Germany I felt the need to go to him. I entered a queue and the Entity invited me to take part in the "current". I was overwhelmed with intense joy and I felt God's presence – in whom I always believed, but who had always been distant. I felt the need to go to Abadiânia where contact with the Entity helped my faith to grow. As I speak many languages I was invited by the organizers to help in the medium João's next visit to Germany.

Result – What happened with me was wonderful. I found inner peace. From the first day of attendance by the Entity my life changed completely. I was also united with God: He was and had always been inside me, but only from that day on I was able to feel Him, hear Him, and love Him truly. Nowadays love, generosity, and light are part of my life. No health problems concern me because I feel God close to me.

⎸ELSA BIQUES SEVERO

Brazilian, divorced, retired, lives at Setor 05, Qd. EE, Bloco 01, apartment 301, Canoas, Guajuviras (RS).

Health problems – At first I began to feel pain in my breasts. I had a temperature and my breasts were swollen, so I decided to see a doctor. Several exams were performed, including an x-ray of the breasts. The exams revealed serious results and made my doctor extremely worried.

Performed treatment – I was submitted to invisible surgery by the medium João-in-Entity on the same day of consultation. Medications were prescribed and I was to return for surgery review. I returned to Casa de Dom Inácio after review and continued with spiritual treatment.

Result – Following a recommendation by the Entity a new mammography was carried out, and the threatening nodules had completely vanished.

⎸GEISON GABRIEL GROSS

Brazilian, married, mechanic, CPF n. 608020490-87, lives at Rua dos Andradas n. 997, Centro, Campo Bom (RS).

Health problems – Acute Myeloid Leukemia (AML-M2), diagnosed some years ago.

Performed treatment – Four days after diagnosis I was submitted to the first chemotherapy session. A few days later I began to take the medication and the water of Casa de Dom Inácio. My photograph was taken to the Casa by a friend. Saint Ignatius promised to help this son and he really did. The first chemotherapy treatment did not produce good results. During the second treatment I had a "neuroticicity" but without after-effects, which is rare. During the third and fourth attempts I lost a lot of weight, I became weak, and chemotherapy once again failed to produce good results. During the fifth chemotherapy treatment I was interned for a longer period and I was discharged on my birthday, August 11. Chemotherapy sessions came to an end and I had 2% of sick cells. I began to attend the outpatient department and after two months a biopsy was performed and no sick cells were found. In brief, the treatment consisted of chemotherapy for eight months and treatment at Casa de Dom Inácio for a few months.

Result – After the treatment Medicine did not find sick cells in my body anymore. When I was attended by the medium João in Rio Grande do Sul the Entity told me that I was already cured and that I would not need a transplant. From Medicine's point of view I am in the transplant queue and I already have a donor. My month-old baby is now my donor. However I have not been called and I never will be. At present I have leukocytes and low platelets but I do not have the illness. There is a fibrosis inside the marrow which prevents it from sending these blood components to the body.

⌐GISELA-CARIN MÜLER

German, single, nurse, Passport n. 500, emitted in Dusseldorf, Germany, lives at Rua 2, Qd.-2, Lt. 09, Abadiânia (GO).

Health problems – My problem began over thirty years ago and it was diagnosed by my doctor as "anosteosarkom". He gave me three more months to live and wanted to amputate my left leg; however he gave up on amputation and began to treat me with radiotherapy. I carried on with my life but some years ago a generalized intoxication spread all over my body due to the radiotherapy. I felt incredible pain and I could only move about with the help of crutches, walking sticks, and wheelchairs. Due to fragility in the bones doctors once again wanted to amputate my leg. I already resided in Abadiânia and recently suffered a serious fall. Months later I had a perforation on the stomach wall and was hospitalized for some time.

Performed treatment – When I heard about Casa de Dom Inácio from a friend who had benefited from spiritual healing I went to Abadiânia for the first time some five years ago. I did not feel any pain during the trip. As I passed by the

Entity and tried to explain my health problem, she said she already knew everything about it. I was submitted to the first spiritual surgery. After the second surgery I did not need crutches or wheelchairs anymore. The Entity told me to return after three months. I did not return in the stipulated time because I own two companies in Germany and business was not going well. My health problem returned with more intensity and I started using crutches once again. I left the companies and traveled to Abadiânia. I was once again submitted to surgery and the crutches were removed. I walked a little unsteadily at first but my condition gradually improved until I was able to ride a bike. Due to my fall I began to meditate on the meaning of life. As my condition gradually improved I began attending Casa de Dom Inácio again and taking part in the "current". When I was ill in bed my son consulted the Entity on my health condition and she told him that she was taking good care of me. In fact no other organs were affected and the exam results were the best possible.

Result – Nowadays my body is strong once again and my leg has almost healed. I do not feel any pain. The period during which I underwent treatment for the stomach perforation served to increase my faith in God. I am happy, full of love, and thankful to all the Entities at Casa de Dom Inácio and to the medium João.

ILVE ANA GIORDANI CHIES

Brazilian, married, housewife, ID n. 8037891242-SSP/RS, CPF n. 212.826.680-72, born September 21, 1948, lives at Rua Elisa Tramontina, 462, Centro, Carlos Barbosa (RS).

Health problems – I suffered from spinal column deviation, widely known as "parrot beak", as well as wear and tear of the seventh vertebra. Therefore I felt intense pain which even reached my eyes. I could not even hold objects because of the weakness in my hands. I was submitted to a wide range of exams with several doctors, all of which stated that my problem was degenerative and related to age. They prescribed only physiotherapy and tranquilizers.

According to one of the doctors, the only solution to my problem would be a surgical procedure for the placing of a new vertebra of considerable cost. There were yet more problems especially aesthetic ones, such as the excess of teeth on the lower arcade which demanded the extraction of the central incisor and the use of braces with a predicted accommodation of three years.

Performed treatment – One day an acquaintance of mine told me he was undergoing treatment at Casa de Dom Inácio regarding a problem in his foot which had broken some time before. I grew curious as I was told that the medium João Teixeira performed long-distance cures and that all that was needed was a photograph of the sick person. I gave a photograph of myself to this acquaintance and, after a few days, he returned and brought with him some medication and the photograph; on the back of it the letter "X" had been written, which indicated that I would have to be submitted to a mediumistic surgery. After taking the prescribed medication I went to Casa de Dom Inácio, where I was submitted to an invisible surgery by the Entities Dr. Augusto de Almeida and Sister Scheilla through the mediation of the medium João Teixeira. I felt all the symptoms and effects of a conventional surgery, such as pains, strong smell of medication, nausea, weakness etc. After the eighth day I felt the Entities working on my body. They removed the stitches and since then have never stopped working on my body by improving, healing, and constantly rejuvenating it. My central incisor was extracted and I started to wear the recommended braces.

Result – I feel 98% cured. I seldom feel slight pain, but all I have to do is drink fluidified water and make a compress with it for the pain to vanish instantly. I am already capable of taking care of my house normally without any difficulties and of body movements which had been impossible in the past. The predicted accommodation for the dental arcade – slow in theory – occurred rapidly. In aesthetic terms stains on my hands vanished, as well as warts, scars, and eyebrow imperfections. My eyesight and hearing also improved considerably.

⎧IRVANETE DA SILVA OLIVEIRA

Brazilian, married, house maid, ID n. 09668197-8 SEPC-RJ, CPF n. 991.836.687-72, lives at Rua 16, n. 64, Cruzeiro 2, Pinheiral (RJ).

Problemas de saúde – I suffered from toxoplasmosis and because of it I lost my right eyesight. I saw doctors in Rio de Janeiro and I was vaccinated but I did not get better. I felt belly aches and had vaginal infection. I sought a doctor who solicited a pelvic ultrasound scan, which revealed the following results: right and left ovaries, measuring 27x26x31 mm on longitudinal, anteroposterior, and transverse axis, respectively; regular and well-defined contours, normal solid homogeneous texture. With such results the doctor said he would operate on me because the Fallopian tubes were blocked and the ovaries would need to be extracted. There was a possibility of high-risk pregnancy.

Performed treatment – When I sought Casa de Dom Inácio I was submitted to an eye surgery at first, and soon after that I began to see light and colors. The Entity told me to return for surgery review. Before review the problems returned and the doctor decided to operate. I returned to Casa de Dom Inácio and the Entity who attended me in the morning decided to operate on my ovaries and my eyesight in the afternoon. In the afternoon the Entity placed his hand on my belly and meanwhile operated on my eyes with a knife and said: "You may carry her away because the daughter has also been operated on her ovaries". I was taken to the recovery room. As soon as spiritual anesthesia wore off I felt nauseated, kept calling my mother deliriously, and vomited blood. But all was well in the end. After forty days I returned to the doctor in Rio de Janeiro and told him that I would not take the medications he had prescribed anymore or be submitted to surgery because the medication was not doing me any good and I had already been spiritually operated on my ovaries. The doctor laughed and did not believe what I said. He then solicited another pelvic ultrasound scan.

Result – The ultrasound scan revealed non-visualized ovaries (surgical) as a result. The doctor who performed the ultrasound scan added the following sentence: ID – absence of ovaries. Therefore spiritual surgery was verified.

⌈JOANNIS STYLIANOS MYLONAS

Greek, naturalized Brazilian, born in the city of Agrinion (Greece) on November 23, 1927, single, retired, ID n. 068.694-SSP/DF, CPF n. 072.730.021-00, lives at SGAN, Qd. 913, Módulo F, Apto. 108, Associação dos Ex-Combatentes do Brasil (Association of Brazil's Ex-combatants), Asa Norte, Brasília (DF).

Health problems – Approximately 28 years ago a wound appeared on the left extremity of my lower lip. During eight years it caused me considerable pain and often opened up like a flower, expelling raw flesh and a white liquid. I was submitted to several exams by doctors in Brasília, all of which had different opinions on the problem and prescribed different medicines and ointments. Some of them stated that it was an incurable disease, whereas others declared that it was syphilis or cancer. I spent a lot of money but I could never be cured, quite the contrary, my condition worsened as the wound progressed. In short, I was embarrassed to talk with others due to the occasionally unbearable smell which exhaled from the wound.

Performed treatment – One day I was taken by a friend to be attended by a skinny, tall, and young "healer" in the satellite city of Gama (Brasília). The Entity – through the medium – told me that the disease would be pulled out by the root. During the surgery she used a small pair of scissors with blunt points, placed it close to the wound without touching it, and made two gestures as if cutting the wound (operating on). I did not feel anything and I did not believe in anything either. I was incredulous because I had given up hope of cure due to statements of many renowned doctors and scientists and, besides, only two cutting-like gestures were made, without any kind of pretension.

Result – About six days later a scab was formed on the wound which fell on its own, and a new layer of skin appeared on the affected region. I was declared completely healed. From then on I never felt any more pain and my mouth is normal nowadays, as if it had never suffered from any ailment. People who see me are quite impressed and immediately want to know what I did in order to heal from that disease. I never heard of Mr. João Teixeira again after the invisible surgery until I recently came across him by mere coincidence. This happened when I was acting as an interpreter to a group of Greeks who came to Brazil for health treatments. This group was already familiar with cures performed by Mr. Teixeira due to international publications. I was asked to accompany the group without knowing that I would be taking it to be treated by the medium João Teixeira, who had healed me in the past. When I arrived in Abadiânia at Casa de Dom Inácio and saw Mr. João Teixeira I was overwhelmed, for I already knew him and was familiar with his mediumistic ability. I was extremely happy to see him again; I had been healed through him long before, in the time when the satellite city of Gama was no more than a suburban area of Brasília, filled with wood constructions and devoid of any infra-structure whatsoever. Nowadays I am very happy to be alive, healthy, strong, and active, filled with joy and gratitude. I wish Mr. Teixeira from the bottom of my heart great strength, vigor, and vitality so that he may continue taking care of sick people for a long time to come.

JOHN FRIESWIJK

New Zealander, born in Auckland, New Zealand, on March 29, 1962, Passport n. L937806, checked by the Brazilian Embassy in Wellington, capital of New Zealand, n. C-0528577, lives at Cape Barrier Road, RD I, Great Barrier Island, New Zealand.

Health problems – Some years ago I became aware of signs of a terrible illness. I often woke up wanting to throw up. I went to the doctor several times and I was told that I was suffering from depression caused by my work and by the sad separation from my partner. Then one day a brain tumor was diagnosed. My family and I were devastated. The doctor told me that it was the biggest brain tumor he had ever seen. I was submitted to a brain surgery at Auckland Hospital and I was later informed that I had been resuscitated twice during surgery. After the operation I was submitted to strong doses of radiotherapy for six weeks, and I became very ill due to the prescribed drugs. Then the tumor stabilized for a while. About a year later, on one of my visits to Auckland Hospital, I was informed that the tumor had begun to grow once again and that if doctors decided to try a new surgery, it would be paralyzed for good or I would die. I felt completely destroyed and defeated when I heard such news. I called for help, by telephone, to many hospitals in the world, but without any success. I liked to dive but doctors told me that I would never be able to dive again and that I would die within three minutes if I did.

Performed treatment – I heard from a friend of the existence of Casa de Dom Inácio. My friend lent me a video tape and, after watching it, I decided to travel to Brazil and seek Casa de Dom Inácio in Abadiânia. I was an extremely weak, sick man then. I was submitted to my first surgery and I felt an amazing sensation. When the Entity was asked whether I should return to Abadiânia she answered that I would return when I felt ready. I did return and received a new operation. The Entity recommended some conducts, all of which were followed: visits to the crystal table, sessions at the spiritual waterfall, dips in the lake with water from the waterfall etc.

Result – After the first surgery I was able to ride and walk normally without feeling any pain. I am eternally grateful to God and pray that I keep on trying to be a better person in this world.

Observation: this statement was made at a registry office and was translated by Mr. João Vasco Pinto Ramos, born in Angola on November 9, 1972, student, owner of the Identity Card of National Citizen issued by the Portuguese Republic, n. 9859616, on February 18, 2000 in Lisbon, lives at Rua Vasco Santana, n. 04, Third District, Postal Code n. 26-85-245, Portela, Loures, Portugal.

JONY RINGO DA CONCEIÇÃO PEREIRA

Brazilian, single, student, born October 6, 1987, son of José Pereira dos Santos and Marlúcia Joana da Conceição Pereira, ID n. 2572817/SSP-DF, lives at QNO 16, Conjunto 37, Casa 9, Ceilândia Norte (DF).

Health problems – According to my mother's account my health problems began when I was one year and five months old and I was operated on in order to remove a "cyst" which was lodged at the end of my spinal column (coccyx). This cyst measured about half a centimeter and since then I began to have several health problems, especially related to vision, hearing, and allergy. My eyes were yellowish and I could not hear noise. I had a chronic allergy which was especially revealed in my eyes and my arms were shorter than normal. Several doctors were consulted but no cure was obtained for all these problems. Despite my age (I was about nine years old at the time), I remember perfectly that during a medical appointment the ophthalmologist told my mother in my presence that I would not grow more than 1,30 m, that I would never be able to have children or lead a normal life. This ophthalmologist worked at Hospital de Base in Brasília and he was highly qualified and respected professionally. He said there was no cure for the problem in my eyes: I was going to become blind. The doctor also told my mother that if she believed in God, she should seek an alternative kind of treatment because Medicine could do nothing for me.

Performed treatment – My mother used to attend Casa de Dom Inácio, where she was healed of epilepsy. Sometimes she took me with her. On one of her visits, after I had given up hope of cure by Medicine and as she was attended by the medium João-in-Entity, he opened my eyes and looked intently into them. At this moment my mother begged the Entity to heal me. The answer was: "I have just operated on him and he will be fine".

Result – From that moment on I got better and better. After seven years I can see normally, my arms and legs have normal length, I do not have allergy, and I attend school normally. In short, I lead a normal life. I still attend Casa de Dom Inácio together with my mum and my sisters and my health keeps getting better.

Observation: these statements were made in the presence of Jony's mother (Marlúcia Joana da Conceição Pereira – ID-SSPDF n. 490.654) and that of his sisters, who confirmed the whole story.

JOSÉ SIQUEIRA BARROS

Brazilian, judicially separated, veterinary doctor, ID n. 01123571-0 IFP/RJ, CIC 240.604.297-91, lives at Rua Itapiru, 155, Bl. Q, Apt. 108, Rio de Janeiro (RJ).

Health problems – I was submitted to a surgery of cardiac revascularization in Rio de Janeiro. After the surgery I began to reveal a stroke of one fourth in the pericardium. A puncture was performed at the Army's Central Hospital, in which approximately 800 ml of liquid were removed, and another stroke occurred. It was diagnosed by radiography carried out at Rio de Janeiro's Military Policlinic and by Doppler echocardiogram. I was treated with diuretics, corticosteroids, and anti-inflammatory drugs, but there was no regression. After another bidimensional echocardiogram with Doppler fluxometry was performed it revealed that the stroke was hard to access by puncture. Therefore cardiologists concluded that there was nothing they could do and that I should wait for the stroke to disappear in time because there was a risk of tamponade. The strokes captured in the various echocardiograms were classified as moderated to important. The seriousness of my condition led to the decision made by a superior medical board which considered me invalid for military service due to my need of constant ambulatorial and hospital assistance.

Performed treatment – A neighbor suggested that I travel to Abadiânia, where his wife had been operated on due to biliary vesicle. I went to Casa de Dom Inácio, where I was submitted to spiritual treatment.

Result – One week after attendance at Casa de Dom Inácio another echocardiogram was performed, and this time I was considered cured according to the following diagnostic: "Reduction in magnitude of pericardic stroke of light degree, with posterior and laminar predominance in the anterior region". Another exam carried out months later revealed that the cure of the stroke remained unchanged in relation to the previous exam.

JOSÉ WILMAR FERNANDES CARNEIRO

Brazilian, married, military officer, ID n. 408.981 issued by the Ministry of Aeronautics, CIC n. 010.009.263-20, lives at Rua Vicente Leite, n. 200, Apt. 103, Bairro Meireles, Fortaleza (CE).

Health problems – I was submitted to exams in Fortaleza (CE) whose results revealed lymphoma of the stomach, both in the endoscopy and in the biopsy. I was informed, together with my family (including my son who is a resident doctor in Brasília), that my condition was very serious and that I was going to be submitted to a treatment by chemotherapy. I knew that this treatment would not solve the problem so I decided not to be submitted to it.

Performed treatment – After obtaining information from others about Casa de Dom Inácio I went to Abadiânia. At first I was attended by the Entity and it told me to return three more times. Medication was prescribed for me. At the end of a month of treatment I returned to the Casa every week and I had put on 1,5 kg (I had lost 20 kg after another stomach surgery for the extraction of a large ulcer a year before). After another month of taking the medication I put on three more kilos. I returned to Abadiânia and the Entity told me to continue taking the medication and return after thirty days.

Result – On my last return visit to Casa de Dom Inácio the Entity told me that I was cured. I returned to Fortaleza and decided to do new exams in the same laboratory as before. The exams revealed that all I had was gastritis and that the illness which had been detected before no longer existed.

JULI BROWN

Irish, single, house agent, born August 13, 1974, lives at Clonsilla Road, Dublin, Ireland.

Health problems – At the age of thirty I went to see a doctor due to health problems. It was a shocking diagnostic: breast cancer. It was an aggressive type of cancer and the tumor was very big. I was submitted to five sessions of generic chemotherapy and fifteen sessions of specific chemotherapy (Merceptin), which resulted in side effects typical of chemotherapy.

Performed treatment – I traveled to Brazil months later in order to visit João de Deus. When I was being attended the Entity told me to "sit in the current" twice. Three sessions of "crystal bath" were also prescribed. After that I was submitted to an invisible surgery and I followed all instructions in the following forty days.

Result – I returned to Ireland and I was submitted to new exams. When my doctor saw my exam results he was happy and, without understanding what had happened, told me that I was "free from the illness". The cancer had vanished.

LAURA VIEIRA DE FREITAS

Brazilian, single, housewife, ID n. M-1.046.207 – SSP/MG, CIC n. 126.128.206-04, lives at Rua Itaguá, 420, Ipanema, Belo Horizonte (MG).

Health problems – My granddaughter Gláucia Vieira Cardoso, when she was ten years old, had a renal cyst type E, which measured 2,1 x 4 centimeters in larger diameters. The cyst was confirmed by exams carried out by specialists.

Performed treatment – I found out about the existence of Casa de Dom Inácio in a conversation with friends and I decided to take my granddaughter to Abadiânia. She was submitted to a spiritual surgery and received some medicines. She returned for review the following month.

Result – After she was submitted to a new series of exams at the same hospital as before and by the same specialists, it was concluded that all was normal for her age and that there was no renal cyst.

LUCINDA JOSEFINA DE TONI SARTORI

Brazilian, married, educational counselor, born April 10, 1940, ID n. 7003994725/RS, CIC n. 466.354.750-87, lives at Av. Presidente Lucena n. 1659, Bairro Harmonia, Ivoti (RS).

Health problem – Some years ago I began to feel symptoms of an illness which was preventing me from performing any kind of activity, even the simplest ones. I felt unable to make any physical effort, I could not even dance or walk quickly. As I suffered from palpitations, pressure fall, dizziness, and intense weakness, I suspected that the illness was related with the heart. Therefore I sought a cardiologist who solicited an electrocardiogram. However, nothing abnormal was observed. Because palpitations occurred frequently I went to two other cardiologists and I was submitted to two other electrocardiograms. Once again nothing abnormal was observed. Afterwards I had a palpitation attack for a period of approximately fifteen days. I was submitted to an echocardiogram which detected the cause of the illness as "free mitral valve prolapse with minimal insufficiency". Despite the apparent simplicity of the name it caused me huge problems. A medication called Angiopress was prescribed and should be taken for the rest of my life. I became worried because I was already taking two other medicines.

Performed treatment – Being a medium I already knew about Casa de Dom Inácio. I was submitted to a preparatory treatment. I was attended by the Entity Dr. Osvaldo Cruz, who told me I would be submitted to an afternoon surgery that very day, which occurred in an invisible way.

Result – I was traveling with an excursion bus so I remained in Abadiânia for three days. As soon as I went back home I noticed an improvement. Fifteen days later I was able to return to my normal activities. I recovered quickly and

I am a healthy person once again. I am now able to carry out all my activities, even those which demand physical effort. I did another echocardiogram which confirmed my complete cure. I feel obliged to register this:

> It is gratifying for me to know that I have a heart within me that beats perfectly. At each beat of my heart I always think back on the grace I received through the Entities at Casa de Dom Inácio and through the medium João.

LUZIA FERNANDES PEREIRA

Brazilian, lives with partner, farm laborer, born January 5, 1941, ID n. M - 7.262.681-SSP/MG, CPF n. 877.227.046-20, lives at Fazenda Nova Lagoa Rica, Lt. 17, Paracatu (MG).

Health problems – Some years ago I started to feel strong pains on the upper left region of my back. Therefore I went to Paracatu Hospital (MG) and I was examined by doctors. An x-ray revealed a black spot on my lung. As the hospital did not offer adequate treatment doctors referred me to Hospital de Base in Brasília (DF). At this hospital I was submitted to several exams, including biopsy, and doctors concluded that I had lung cancer in an advanced stage. The following report was issued and signed by a doctor:

Mrs. Luzia Fernandes Pereira, 58, HBDF record n. 863.149, was interned in our unit from October 21 to November 25 of this year with a diagnosis of lung cancer. The patient was submitted to cervical mediastinoscopy for staging, with biopsy of paratracheal lymphonodes, whose histopathological diagnostic consists of metastatic carcinoma (lung adenocarcinoma) for mediastinal lymphonodes (biopsy n. 7316/99 - HBDF). The stage of the illness contraindicates surgical treatment, therefore the patient is referred to clinic oncology for complementary treatment.

I remained for over a month at Hospital de Base in Brasília treating this terrible illness, during which I was submitted to an urgent surgery of the thorax. Due to the illness's advanced stage the doctors gave up hope of cure because the tumor continued to grow despite the treatment, which indicated that there were no more chances of recovery.

Performed treatment – As I had been cured of a nervous ulcer and a uterine infection in the past through invisible surgery at Casa de Dom Inácio, I went to see the medium João Teixeira once again. When I arrived in Abadiânia my health condition was terrible. After the first consultation and after I took the prescribed medication I began to feel better. I returned to Casa de Dom Inácio several times for invisible surgery.

Result – I am now completely healed, I have gone back to work in the plantation normally, and I cook for laborers at the rice harvest without feeling anything abnormal.

MARCILENE DA SILVA OLIVEIRA REIDER

Brazilian, married, housewife, ID n. 604.602-2.ª Via – DGPC, CPF n. 664.010.111-49, lives at Rua Trindade, Qd. 46, Lt. 08, Parque João Braz, Goiânia (GO).

Health problems – It all began a few years ago when "lumps" appeared on my breasts and on my left arm. The lumps on my arm turned into wounds that did not heal and gradually increased, and I was losing arm movements. I had several appointments with different doctors but the illness failed to be diagnosed. I was referred to doctors at the University of São Paulo (USP/SP) who concluded after thorough exams that I had a rare illness called "Faicete Esonomolofique" and there were only three similar cases in Brazil. I was submitted to approximately ten surgeries for the removal of nerves in the left arm, but to no avail. The pain increased, arm movements disappeared, and surgery cuts did not heal. Doctors of the University of São Paulo told me there was no possibility of cure and that my left arm needed to be amputated.

Performed treatment – On my first spiritual appointment the medium João-in-Entity said that my arm did not have to be amputated and that he would help me.

A charitable person came to know of my personal drama and paid for my travel expenses to Abadiânia[62]. I was given four boxes of phytotherapic tablets which I began to take immediately. On the first week after I began to take the medication I felt a significant improvement. The pain lessened, arm movements returned, and surgery cuts began to heal.

Result – After forty days, following a recommendation by the Entity, I returned to Casa de Dom Inácio for a new spiritual appointment; by then I was practically healed, I did not feel pain, and my arm had recovered almost entirely. I traveled to Abadiânia many times and my recovery was more and more complete. I had lost the movement of my arm and I could not even brush my hair, but nowadays I can move it and I lead a normal life. I am cured and I do not feel any pain. The charitable person whom God placed on my path still pays for my trips to Abadiânia. Whenever I show color photographs of the horrible wounds I had on my arm people feel sick just by looking at them. Doctors told me that the wounds would never heal, and now they have healed completely. As far as being able to move my arm after nerves were extracted, there is no scientific explanation that accounts for it.

| MÁRIO JÚLIO MELO DE CARVALHO

Portuguese, married, chief inspector of Portugal's Judiciary Police (a Police Superior Board which has some similarities with the Brazilian Federal Police and USA's FBI), Passport E-561082, lives at Rua Moinho de Cima, 19, Vale de Santarém, Portugal.

Health problems – Years ago a specialist in gastroenterology in Lisbon diagnosed an adenocarcinoma in my large intestine, in other words in the colon located in the sigmoid zone. This cancer was already in an intermediary stage, with vascular invasions and five metastases in the mesentery which covered that part of the colon. Curiously,

---

[62] The person in question, Heather MacDonald Cumming, is a Brazilian guide.

months before, Mr. João Teixeira de Faria had visited Portugal and had told me that I needed to go to Abadiânia. However, I only considered (I was a skeptic at the time) a visit to Casa de Dom Inácio necessary in a situation of extreme seriousness, a situation which I believed would never happen. I was submitted to a surgery at a clinic in Lisbon, where 20 cm of the colon were removed. Due to already existing complications six months of preventive chemotherapy were prescribed.

Performed treatment – My wife, moved by religious conviction, went to Casa de Dom Inácio and took a picture of me with her. The Entity who attended her said: "This son has to come to Abadiânia urgently". This happened before the surgery in Lisbon. I only traveled to Brazil after the surgery. At Casa de Dom Inácio I was spiritually operated on by the Entity Dr. Augusto Almeida, who said at the end of the procedure: "Son, now you have been operated on and you may go". I remained in Abadiânia for three weeks attending Casa de Dom Inácio. As the days went by I felt better and I experienced feelings of peace, tranquility, and faith which I had never felt before. It is my profound conviction that the hand of God, through His Entities of Light, guided the hand of the human surgeon and the oncologist who treated me with chemotherapy during long months.

Result – I can now declare, after obtaining exam results and having concluded the chemotherapy treatment, that the cancer which attacked me was overcome and defeated.

MAURO COSTA

Brazilian, single, retired, ID n. 1-R – 192.586 – SSP/SC, CPF n. 341.566.319-15, lives at Rua Príncipe, 276, Bairro Saco Grande II, Florianópolis (SC).

Health problems – Years ago I worked at the barracks of the Military Police in Florianópolis and one day I felt a sharp pain on my right leg as I went down some stairs. Despite the pain I continued down the stairs until the pain became too great and I fell. I was helped by colleagues who took me to the police hospital. The doctors placed a splint on my leg and asked me to return for my leg to be plastered.

It was plastered many times. While my leg was plastered the pain lessened, whereas it returned with great intensity as soon as the plaster was removed. Afterwards I was asked to undergo a medical evaluation. I walked with the aid of crutches and the medical evaluation indicated a surgery which did not have positive results. After the surgery I no longer felt my legs and I lost all sensitivity from the waist down. I did physiotherapy and I was referred from one doctor to the next without any solution to the problem. Tired of exams, I went to the Sara Kubitschek Hospital in Brasília, where I remained for 28 days. An apparatus was placed on my leg for testing and soon after I was told that, unfortunately, there was no solution to my problem.

Performed treatment – I left the Sara Kubitschek Hospital crying and completely desperate when suddenly I was approached by a woman who advised me to seek Casa de Dom Inácio, because if it did not do any good, no harm would come from it either. I decided to go to Abadiânia despite my almost complete lack of money. I had no idea of which direction to take. I bought a ticket at the bus station and I asked a woman inside the bus where she was heading. Then she told me that she was heading for Abadiânia, so I was relieved. She informed me that she lived on the same street as Casa de Dom Inácio and from then on she gave me all the information I needed. I was alone, with little money, using crutches, and carrying a backpack. I arrived at Casa de Dom Inácio at about 5 pm and I was attended at once. Only medicines were prescribed and I received the recommendation to return after the medication finished. I found a pension and I explained my situation. The pension owner told me that I could stay on for forty days until I finished the medication. On the following week I heard of surgeries performed at Casa de Dom Inácio and I went back there. As I did not know about procedures I entered one of the queues and passed by the Entity, who said: "Son, you have not finished the medication yet, but come back tomorrow at eight o'clock and I will operate on you". The next day, as I entered the surgery room I felt numbness in my whole body and I fell, but without losing consciousness. I had half fainted and I heard someone say: "Bring this son forward". My movements returned but my legs remained paralyzed. The Entity said: "Son, come back at 2 o'clock for I want to see you". I returned at 2 pm and when I was getting close to the Entity I felt numbness over my entire body and I fell again. The Entity asked me to sit in the current near her and to place the crutches by the wall. Once I had sat down a young woman told me to close my eyes and pray.

Result – When I opened my eyes there was almost nobody left in the room; only two young men were behind me, as I had slept for about five hours. I woke up, got up, and walked out rather unsteadily. One of the young men asked if I wanted the crutches and I said no, because I did not remember that I used them. As I left the house two young women found me, hugged me, and went to the pension with me, remarking that I did not use crutches anymore. I took about fifteen days to get used to the absence of the crutches. People on an excursion from Rio Grande do Sul bought me some shoes because I did not have any and made a detour in their route in order to take me home to Florianópolis. Once there a neighbor who saw me without crutches and walking normally fainted. From then on I have not had any more problems and I can walk normally as well as make any movement whatsoever.

| MIGUEL VIEDMA

Swiss, born May 25, 1956, married, reflexologist, Passport n. I.D. C0510235, issued in Geneva, lives at 3 B, Rue de La Gare – 1196, Gland (Geneva), Switzerland.

Health problems – I was three years old when a cyst (small tumor) appeared on my left arm, on the deltoid muscle.

Performed treatment – Years ago I was operated on by the Entity Augusto de Almeida. The operation did not involve anesthesia or asepsis. It did not hurt and there was no infection. After the cyst was removed two plasters were placed on the area for protection. This surgery was performed in the presence of more than fifteen people, among them a doctor and my wife; there were over 700 people awaiting attendance. The process lasted approximately twenty minutes.

Result – There is nothing wrong with me, all that remained is a small scar. I am deeply grateful to the Entity and to the medium João.

NADIR GUMIERO LENA

Brazilian, married, housewife, ID n. M-2.884.181-SSP/MG, CIC n. 031.916.197-80, lives at Rua Messias Gonçalves Correia, n. 115, Bairro Nossa Senhora da Penha, Vila Velha (ES).

Health problem – A solid nodule on my right breast, detected in a routine ultrasound scan. I did not attend the medical recommendation of doing a biopsy, I abandoned the conventional treatment, and went in search of a spiritual one.

Performed treatment – On the first consultation the Entity said that I would undergo surgery on that same afternoon, which was done in an invisible way. I took the prescribed medication (Passiflora).

Result – An initial mammography revealed that the nodule had moved from the upper external right quadrant to the lower quadrant. The second mammography of high resolution did not detect any nodule. I keep the exams which were carried out before and after the spiritual treatment.

NARA VIRGÍNIA FRAGA SILVA

Brazilian, divorced, state public worker, ID n. 4005038701-SSP/RS, CIC n. 168.522.140-87, lives at Rua Xangrilá, 147, Parque Jaqueline, Gravataí (RS).

Health problems – Some years ago I began to feel strong pains around the liver region. I consulted with many doctors for eight consecutive years, all of which solicited various exams, such as tomography, echography, and cintilography. All these exams were in vain because nothing was detected. A gynecologist told me to be submitted to a laparoscopy which demanded a small surgery, with an incision and the introduction of apparatus to visualize internal organs.

The exam was carried out and the doctor was shocked with the state of the organs, all were joined together. One could not define the organs, distinguish them from each other or even separate them. Based on this diagnostic and in order to reduce the constant pains, seventeen surgeries were performed for the removal of adherences and especially for the liberation of the liver due to violent pains. I took morphine for a year and two months in order to bear the pain. The specialist doctor told me that there was no hope of cure in Brazil or abroad and advised me to seek an alternative treatment if I believed in it.

Performed treatment – Some days later I was feeling anguished at a beach in Santa Catarina when I felt horrible pains. A woman approached me and started talking to me. She asked me what I was feeling and I told her of all that I had been through in the last few years. The woman then started talking about Casa de Dom Inácio in Abadiânia and about the work performed by the medium João. I returned to Porto Alegre and when I visited my father I met the woman who took care of him. She had found out she had cancer in the intestine and would therefore travel to Abadiânia, so I decided to go with her. After arriving in Abadiânia, on my first consultation, the Entity told me without prior knowledge about my health that I would be cured, despite having given up hope of cure due to the statements of doctors. The surgery was set for the following day and I was indeed operated on.

Result – The surgery healed wonderfully well and from that moment on I have never felt any more pain. My gynecologist declared the cure and she even remarked: "Look at you now". My cure was proved. On my fourth visit to Casa de Dom Inácio the Entity told me that I should do for others what had been done for me. Therefore I started to organize excursions to Abadiânia. Personally I know of several cures received by people who traveled in my excursions. I can cite cures of several illnesses, including hydrocephalia, spinal amiotrophy of type II, facial paralysis, facial cancer, breast cancer, lump in the bone marrow, and cancer of the uterus.

| OLIVO GHELER

Brazilian, married, retired, ID n. 2.274.973, Instituto Félix Pacheco – RJ, CPF n. 227.827.707-30, lives at Rua V-8, Qd. V-15, Lt. 16-A, Vila Rezende, Goiânia (GO).

Health problems – Parkinson's disease. Years ago a neurologist diagnosed the illness. It was a terrible shock to me. I considered myself too young for it. In fact I had been feeling the symptoms for about two years. It all began with some tiny pulls on the middle finger of my left hand while I went on walks. I became even more disappointed after I read about the illness: completely harmful, incurable, degenerative, progressive, debilitating. I felt even more impotent when I read two Reader's Digest publications, which declared that a NASA engineer and a Hollywood actor also suffered from Parkinson's disease but did not obtain a cure, despite the financial and clinic conditions of these American citizens. After discovering that I had the illness I greatly wished to seek the medium João de Deus at Casa de Dom Inácio in Abadiânia. I thought: "If I have faith, I will be cured" and faith was something which I did not lack. My wife and I paid our first visit to the good medium. I consulted with him in the morning and I was operated on in the afternoon. I followed all instructions and I took the medication. I return regularly for review and in order to obtain more medicines.

Performed treatment – The performed treatment consisted of a spiritual surgery parallel to clinical treatment, which included return visits to Casa de Dom Inácio for reviews since its beginning. I intend to continue with this treatment until the medium João de Deus discharges me and tells me that I do not have to return to Casa de Dom Inácio anymore.

Result – I consider myself cured. As a result I may safely say that I am about 90% cured, and I take medication provided by Casa de Dom Inácio and other medicines prescribed by Earth doctors. I have been informed that my problem is under control, it has not progressed anymore. I have to say that I took the decision of greatly reducing the ingestion of these medicines and it did not affect involuntary movements. This decision was taken after a second spiritual surgery took place at the Casa about six months ago.

⎸PEDRO ANDRIOLLE BEDIM

Brazilian, widow, retired, ID n. 3.068.029-4/PR, lives at Rua Levino Zeni, 241, Capitão Leônidas Marques (PR).

Health problems – Years ago a cancer appeared on the left side of my face. Symptoms began in the face and spread out to the body; I started feeling stomachache, pain on the left side of the body, and several lumps on the scalp. I could not be exposed to the sun because the pain increased.

Performed treatment – The treatment began in the same year and lasted eleven years. I visited Casa de Dom Inácio every 45 days. During the first five years there was no spiritual surgery, only treatment with energy. More than thirty surgeries were performed in the last six years.

Result – From the first medication on I did not feel any more pain. Recently the Entity told me that I was healed and that I could be submitted to a corrective surgery on the left side of my face. The surgery was performed without any after effects.

⎸REGINA WILLIAMS

North American, born in Pittsburgh, Pennsylvania, United Sates of America, single, retired, American Passport n. 09550411, issued in May 2001, lives at Rua Tereza, Qd. G, Lt. 04, Vila Bastos, Abadiânia (GO).

Health problems – While in the USA I went on a diet during twelve months. I took medication which was later removed from the market because it was killing people. Before starting the diet I had good health and I led a normal and very active life. After the use of the medication I began to breathe with difficulty and my body began to swell. I had pneumonia and thus began a series of visits to doctors of twelve different specialties. During treatment I was submitted to horrible exams including cardiac cauterization, which revealed that I was suffering from "mitral prolapse" that caused fibromyalgia and apnea. The twelve doctors tried to help me. They gave me more drugs and did what they could, but they told me that there was no cure for my problem and that my heart would eventually stop beating. As I started to take new medication for lung hypertension an internal kidney bleeding began. My kidneys stopped working and nothing could be done to revert this.

Performed treatment – Some acquaintances took me to Abadiânia. During the first 48 hours the owner of the inn where I was staying had to keep an eye on me every ten minutes because my condition was so serious. She did this in order to make sure that I was breathing, as I was in a wheelchair and breathed with the help of a machine. People said that I would die within the next 24 hours. That was when I went to Casa de Dom Inácio, where the Entities referred me to an invisible surgery and suggested that I remain in Abadiânia even after the rest of the group left. I listened to the Entities and did everything that was asked.

Result – Healing demanded time and patience, but I am alive and back to a normal life. I do not need a wheelchair or a breathing machine. I was saved at Casa de Dom Inácio.

RENY EGIDIO BRUN

Brazilian, married, dental surgeon, ID n. 4020997955-SSP-RS, CPF n. 000.255.770-34, lives at Rua Paissandú, 509, Porto Alegre (RS).

Health problems – Years ago I had an appointment at a private clinic in the city of Porto Alegre (RS). When I got there I was seen by two dermatologists who detected basocellular cancer in my right eye and epidermoid cancer in many parts of my body. I was referred to another doctor for the removal of the tumors and for further laboratorial exams which would confirm or not their removal. As I got home with the flask intended for the exams my wife and my daughter did not allow me to do them. They suggested I go to the Entity in Abadiânia and I accepted their request.

Performed treatment – When the medium João traveled to the city of Santo Ângelo (RS) I tried to consult with him there. I was accompanied by my wife and my daughter Maria Cristina, who requested and even begged the Entity to see me. On that same afternoon I was attended and I was submitted to the first surgery on part of the tumor. On that occasion the incorporated Entity was Dr. Augusto de Almeida, who asked me to go to Abadiânia nine days later for review. And so I did during six months, three days a month. One day the Entity which identified himself as Dr. José Valdivino told me that the work performed by Dr. Augusto de Almeida would be concluded by him with the removal of the remaining part of the tumor. After the surgery he handed me the tissue for subsequent laboratorial exams. In addition he told me that as soon as the reddened aspect vanished from my sight I could do as many exams as I wished in order to confirm the case.

Result – I followed the Entity's recommendation and went to São Camilo Hospital at PUC (Pontifical Catholic University) – Rio Grande do Sul, where I was submitted to all the necessary exams that confirmed the non-existence of any cancer cell whatsoever. Medical reports were presented at a registry office together with the present statement.

⌊RICARDO DEMÉTRIO

Peruvian, married, stonemason, Passport n. 0219909, issued by the Peruvian Embassy, lives at 121 Lewis St. Yankees, New York, 10703, USA.

Health problems – I had a malignant tumor in the region of my right arm and my collar bone in the shape of a well-developed lump. I believe that this tumor originated due to a work accident I had some years ago, when I was hit in that area with a sharp object. The tumor appeared in the scar in the shape of a lump. Therefore I was unable to work or move my right arm. I felt strong pains constantly and I was even unable to sleep. I was submitted to several treatments and five surgeries in New York City (USA). I was operated on for the removal of the tumor but six months later it became stronger and more aggressive. In one of the surgeries a small part of my collar bone was removed and screws were placed, but all was in vain. The tumor progressed and was almost reaching the area of the neck. The only alternative considered by the doctors in order to destroy the tumor would be to amputate my right arm in the affected area.

Performed treatment – As soon as I found out about the existence of Casa de Dom Inácio from my mother – the medium João had traveled throughout Peru and performed true miracles – I went to Abadiânia and I was submitted to my first invisible surgery. I returned to New York soon afterwards still in pain. I continued taking the prescribed medication and two weeks later I began to feel better: there was a change in my way of walking and my body was uprighted to a normal position. I returned to Casa de Dom Inácio and I was submitted to another invisible surgery.

Result – After the second surgery I returned to New York. I did not feel any more pain and I was already able to sleep well. I was completely healed. The lump cannot be seen anymore and the tumor disappeared. After a year I returned to Casa de Dom Inácio for a review and to show that I was in good health. Nowadays, whenever someone who had known me in my former critical state sees me, they have difficulties in believing their eyes and are always visibly surprised.

ROSA DELY BRENNER

Brazilian, married, housewife, CTSP n. 74.372, series 139, CIC n. 218.197.850-68, lives at Rua Itapiru, n. 239, Bairro Guarany com Vila Nova, Novo Hamburgo (RS).

Health problems – I had several heart problems: cardiologists had recommended surgeries for the placing of three saphenous vein grafts because heart veins were blocked. I could not believe it, even though I felt very weak and unable to perform the slightest physical effort. I got tired just by walking fifteen steps. A tumor also appeared on my back; it stung and itched at the same time. I also developed an aggressive allergy on my hands. As I used soap powder with hot water for washing clothes the skin became irritated and blisters began to appear. The blisters itched and stung very much and produced a liquid. After a while they burst, turned into a kind of thick scab, and caused cracks which reached the bone. Therefore I sought many doctors, all of whom suggested I consult with a renowned dermatologist in Novo Hamburgo. This dermatologist examined me and prescribed many medicines. However they did not produce any results. He also performed several exams such as erythrogram, echogram, creatinine, total cholesterol, triglicerids, and uric acid, but nothing abnormal was detected. The treatment with the dermatologist lasted about one year and two months and my hands only got worse. Because of the prescribed medication, the exams, and the absence of regression of my hands' abnormal condition, the specialist told me that there was no other conventional treatment for this illness; all possible and known treatments of conventional medicine had been tested. The doctor implied that my problem could be of a spiritual nature.

Performed treatment – I was submitted to spiritual exams at Casa de Dom Inácio. At first I sought the medium João de Deus out of sheer curiosity. The Entity operated on me as soon as I was attended. However I only found out what kind of operation had been performed on me the following day when I asked the Entity about it. I had a serious heart problem. As I consulted the Entity Dr. Augusto about the tumor on my back he asked me to show it to him and instantly called for a chair so that I could sit down. At that moment he operated on me without any instrument whatsoever. All I felt was a great amount of liquid run down my back which soaked my blouse. Afterwards I was submitted to spiritual exams and the Entity Dr. Augusto performed invisible scrapings on my hands twice. I did not see such scrapings but I felt my hands sting during the procedure.

Result – The health problems which occurred at different times revealed the following results: a) heart: I was completely healed; b) tumor on my back: I rested for two days and was discharged by the Entity soon afterwards; I did not feel pain anymore and I all I took with me were five bottles of medicine. I was completely healed from this illness; c) hand allergy: I took the medication prescribed by the Entity and I unexpectedly began to feel better. A few days later the skin on my hands became smooth and healthy. The dermatologist was very impressed and said that it could only be a miracle of God.

TÂNIA DE FÁTIMA ADREONI

Brazilian, divorced, housewife, ID n. 2005999491, Porto Alegre, Rio Grande do Sul, lives at Rua 02, Quadra 11, lote 07, Bairro Lindo Horizonte, Abadiânia (GO).

Health problems – At first I went to Casa de Dom Inácio for the health treatment of my partner who had retinal degeneration. One morning during a trip from Porto Alegre to Abadiânia I went to the bathroom, fell, and injured my kneecap. At that very moment I felt as if I had been spiritually attended by the Entities at Casa de Dom Inácio. I went to the hospital in Balneário Camboriú in Santa Catarina for an x-ray of the knee, which revealed that my kneecap had broken completely. Immediately the doctor wanted me to be submitted to surgery in order to place a prosthesis with pins connected to the knee because he assumed I was in a lot of pain. I did not feel any pain and I refused to undergo surgery as well as take any kind of medication. I only drank fluidified water and allowed the doctor to place a splint on my leg so I could continue my trip to Abadiânia.

Performed treatment – When I arrived in Abadiânia there was no pain or swelling. I was able to walk without anybody's help and I felt physically well. From that day on I remained in Abadiânia and I became a town resident. I never felt the need to use a walking stick, crutches, or a prosthesis. I was treated exclusively by the Entities at Casa de Dom

Inácio and no doctor touched my knee. A few days later the splint became loose by itself and someone removed it and placed only a bandage on my knee. I walked all over Abadiânia without a kneecap. During the treatment I started doing voluntary work (I helped people at the ward at Casa de Dom Inácio). I read the gospels at home, in inns, and in the homes of those who asked me to. The Entities of the Casa performed many surgeries without my knowledge.

Result – A year after the accident, when I returned to my hometown and consulted an orthopedist, he told me that he could not explain how I could walk about normally without a kneecap. Nowadays I am very happy for the privilege of being a daughter of Casa de Dom Inácio, where I learned the meaning of true love, peace, and happiness, because we all feel the presence of God in our hearts when we are there. I was cured by my faith, by my work as a volunteer, by my love for Casa de Dom Inácio, and by the love shown by the Entities to all those who arrive at the Casa in search of something. I received many graces, not only for myself but for all my family.

ISMAR ESTULANO GARCIA

Brazilian, divorced, lawyer and university professor, 62 years old, ID n. 2399 (OAB-GO), professional address at Avenida Goiás, n. 310, 7° andar, conjunto 701, Goiânia (GO).

Health problems – At the age of fifty the Medical Division of the employing company where I worked, Universidade Católica de Goiás (UCG), recommended a prostate exam at least once a year. I followed the recommendation regularly and PSA results were always normal. At the age of 59 the PSA exam revealed an excessively high rate in contrast with the previous exam carried out six months before. It is worth mentioning that in the four months prior to the exam I had gone through serious personal problems which resulted in certain psychological disorders. The urologist doctor who had been following my exams for years became concerned and passed my case on to a colleague. The latter solicited a prostrate biopsy and the results were alarming: cancer. Further exams were performed by specialists who verified a metastasis. The result of the cintilography confirmed a metastasis on the pelvis. The doctor recommended the extraction of the prostrate in an attempt to improve quality of life only, because the metastasis was irreversible. One of the doctors told me that I should not have much hope because, at the rate at which the illness was spreading, my life expectancy was down to about five years. Another doctor said that many research studies were being carried out all over the world and a cure could be discovered. Yet another doctor uttered a significant sentence: "In many years of my profession I have seen unexplainable things. To God nothing is impossible". Only those who had a similar experience may have an idea of how I felt. I started suffering from insomnia and from periods of complete lack of control for normal daily work. I had an allergy and I had been undergoing treatment with a homeopath for several years. I went to see him and began to feel some sort of psychological tranquility. The homeopath spoke of a friend who was a naturalist doctor and performed alternative treatments which were different from conventional medical treatments. I sought him and treatment began. Improvements were perceptible. Some time later a pelvis biopsy revealed nothing abnormal. The oncologist declared the non-existence of metastasis and opted for the extraction of the prostrate. The naturalist doctor advised me not to go ahead with the surgery because the cancer was receding. I decided not to do the surgery. I began to believe in the alternative treatment and I followed what was prescribed to me, based on controlled diet and natural medicines.

Eleven doctors were consulted in total, but three were not aware that I had cancer. I told them that it was my father who had the illness and that I intended to help him in the best possible way. My aim was to obtain as much information as I could about the illness. All doctors were very honest, especially because I had asked them not to omit anything. Instead of making negative remarks about any of the doctors consulted, I declare that I have the utmost respect and consideration for all of them and for the attendance they provided. They did the best they could within their specialties. I mention only two names: Dr. Carlos Lima Melo (Goiânia - GO) and Dr. Fernando Hoisel (Salvador - BA).

Performed treatment – It was during the period of alternative treatment that I went to Casa de Dom Inácio for the first time, not because of health problems but in a professional capacity. When I was attended for the first time, without having said anything about my illness, the Entity only said that he would help me and prescribed Passiflora, which I took according to the recommendation. On one occasion, as I returned from a trip and had lunch with the medium João at a restaurant, he told me that I had a health problem but that I should not worry about it, for the illness would disappear naturally. Months later, as I took part in procedures at Casa de Dom Inácio, the Entity said he was "taking care" of me. After some time the Entity told me that my work was coming to an end. Even though I had reduced the naturalist medication I had never abandoned it completely.

Result – After some time, after having overcome several doubts and witnessed scientifically unexplainable things, I began to believe in spiritual treatment. After psychological and spiritual recycling I was prepared for the worst. However, to my delight, spiritual treatment changed my life completely. When I finished writing this book I inquired whether my personal problem could be included in the group of real healing stories, and I received authorization to do it. Several years have gone by since the biopsy that detected the metastasis. I feel well and I perform my professional activities normally. Now I am happy and I can say that getting to know the medium João and attending Casa de Dom Inácio was one of the best things that ever happened to me.

⌊JOÃO TEIXEIRA DE FARIA

Brazilian, divorced, farmer, address for contact at Casa de Dom Inácio, Abadiânia (GO).

Health problems – Long ago I had a brain stroke. As a result one of my eyes became crooked, my arms rigid, my hands "loose", and my body a little lopsided. Nevertheless, I continued to attend people at Casa de Dom Inácio and the situation continued for quite some time. The Entities continued to perform spiritual healing using my body as an instrument. As I was told, during incorporation my eye, arms, hands, and body went back to normal and did not show signs of the stroke. However, as soon as I de-incorporated the former situation returned: crooked eye, rigid arms, "loose" hands, and lopsided body.

Performed treatment – When I am incorporated I enter a state which resembles sleep; I do not remember what happens during incorporation. However, I was informed that one day the Entity told all those present that I would be operated on. With the use of my hands a cut was made with a scalpel on my thorax, a little below my left nipple. It is said that I introduced two fingers inside the cut, which was regarded by many as "self-surgery". Apparently there was little blood. I did not feel pain and the cut healed quickly.

Result – I was completely healed. The crooked eye went back to normal and the same happened with my arms, hands, and body. Many years have passed and I continue with my mission of serving as an instrument for good spirits to perform scientifically unexplainable cures.

Chapter VI

Spiritual Manifestations and Brazilian Law

When one deals with juridical topics it is necessary to employ technical terms which are not always understood by most people. The author used the simplest form of language possible in order to avoid difficulties for the reader. For those who apply the law (police chiefs, prosecutors, judges, and lawyers) some explanations hereby included may appear too simple. However, for many others such explanations are necessary to provide a more effective understanding of the topic.

1. Religious freedom

Does the Federal Constitution guarantee religious freedom for the Brazilian citizen?

Yes, especially because there is no freedom without religion and no religion without freedom. It is clearly stated in the Magna Carta of 1988, art. 5, VI: "Freedom of conscience and of belief is inviolable. The free practice of religious cults is secured and protection to places of worship and their liturgies is guaranteed by law."

Based on this constitutional norm would spiritual healing be legally secured as religious freedom?

Yes. Religious freedom is a right of every citizen and it is acknowledged in the majority of judicial decisions. Unfortunately there is a minority who does not think this way.

Is there any norm that is in favor of spiritual healing?

In the case of spiritual healing and as far as the topics discussed here are concerned one cannot talk of crimes. Human laws may only set norms for human conducts. Spiritual healing is still unexplained by science. If one considers the absence of scientific explanations, then the conducts taken to perform spiritual healing are licit.

2. Law

What is Law?

This word may have several meanings. Of all the possible meanings the one that matters will offer the reader a better understanding for the explanations hereby given. Therefore, Law refers to the set of written norms related to a certain subject. In more specific terms related to the aims of this book, Law concerns legal norms which refer to spiritual healing.

In order to understand what Law is, it is necessary to know how it is structured.

In general terms how is Law structured?

Law is basically integrated by law, doctrine, and jurisprudence. As far as the present topic is concerned, law describes conducts which in theory are regarded as licit. The law is in fact Penal Law, which typifies conducts that are considered illegal practice of medicine, charlatanism, and healing. A doctrine[63] comments on these three penal types whereas jurisprudence focuses on the actual position of courts regarding illicit procedures related to spiritual healing.

How does doctrine regard spiritual healing?

In general terms it is in favor of serious spiritual manifestations and respects the constitutional guarantee of religious freedom.

How does jurisprudence regard spiritual healing?

In a similar way. It attempts to establish a difference between what is fraudulent and what is true.

3. Penal Code

Specifically which area of Law focuses on cases related to spiritual healing?

The Penal Code.

What is the Penal Code?

The Penal Code is a collection of articles which establish general punitive norms, criminal conducts, and sentences which apply the right of punishment of the State. It is divided into two parts: the General Part deals with punitive rules in general and the Special Part specifically focuses on conducts which are depicted as crimes. Conducts which are typified as crimes are grouped under titles related to a given juridical good: person, patrimony, immaterial property, labor organization, customs, family, public safety, public administration etc. Specifically under the title 'public safety' there is a chapter concerning public health: epidemic, omission of disease notification, poisoning of drinking water, adulteration of medication, commercialization of substances which are harmful to public health, illegal practice of medicine, charlatanism, healing etc.

---

[63] In the field of Law a 'doctrine' consists of the opinions of lawyers on a given subject.

The law simultaneously describes a conduct regarded as crime and establishes the punishment for the offender. In other words, the Penal Code typifies illicit conducts and establishes, in an abstract way, the sentence to be applied.

What is 'public safety'?

In the field of Law 'public safety' refers to safety which is extended to all citizens without any specification. In short, it consists of public tranquility and social peace. In the present case public safety attempts to prevent danger to the health of an indeterminate number of people.

4. Typification

What does 'to typify' mean?

It means to suit a concrete case to an abstract description or typical conduct prescribed by the Penal Code.

What are typical conducts?

Brazilian legislators have selected several conducts regarded as penal infractions and have catalogued them in what is now conventionally named the Penal Code. The description of a conduct is its penal type. When a certain individual performs an act of agreement with the description that establishes the type of criminal offense it is said that the conduct is typical, in other words, it may be regarded as an infraction. When the analyzed conduct is not adequate, in other words, it fails to meet all the elements of a typical description it is called an atypical conduct and thus does not constitute a crime.

Is it a responsibility of the State to typify conducts described as illicit?

Yes. It is a responsibility of the State to take general measures for the protection of citizens. As far as public health is concerned the State declares the possibility of punishment for certain conducts which may prove harmful to public health, among other norms.

In what way does Brazilian Law approach the topic of spiritual healing?

As previously stated the Law is made up of law, doctrine, and jurisprudence. Penal law typifies as crime certain conducts associated with spiritual healing, but it is up to doctrine (opinions of specialists) and to jurisprudence (court decisions) to analyze and separate what is serious from what constitutes fraud, and this occurs normally. In such violent times no sensible magistrate applies the law by punishing serious individuals who only wish to do good for others without harming anyone.

What does the Penal Code consider as crime as far as spiritual healing is concerned?

Among all the various conducts which are regarded as crimes against public health and are connected to spiritual healing, the Penal Code presents three, which are: illegal practice of medicine – dental or pharmaceutical art –, charlatanism, and healing.

What does each of these allegedly criminal conducts consist of in detail?

It is best to transcribe here how the Penal Code in fact describes each criminal conduct.

Illegal practice of medicine, dental or pharmaceutical art:[64]

To perform, albeit free of charge, the profession of doctor, dentist, or pharmacist without legal authorization or by exceeding its limits:

Sentence – detention from 6 (six) months to 2 (two) years.

Sole paragraph. If the crime is committed for profit, a fine will also be applied.

Charlatanism:[65]

To demonstrate or to announce a cure through secret or infallible means:

Sentence – detention from 3 (three) months to 1 (one) year and a fine.

Healing:[66]

To perform healing by:

I – prescribing, administering, or habitually applying any substance;

II – employing gestures, words, or any other means;

---

[64] Penal Code, art. 282.

[65] Penal Code, art. 283.

[66] Penal Code, art. 284.

III – providing diagnostics:

Sentence – detention from 6 (six) months to 2 (two) years.

Sole paragraph. If the crime is committed for payment the agent is also subject to a fine.

How can one distinguish such crimes in a simple way?

A simple way to distinguish them would be as follows:

a) Illegal practice of medicine: an individual has medical knowledge and may even possess a medical degree; in short, this person may have professional ability but not legal authorization;

b) Charlatanism: false promises of healing are given;

c) Healing: an individual who performs healing is unlearned, simple, rude, and employs rude methods in treatments; this person frequently employs sorcery and cunning and usually makes healing a means to earn a living.

If a given practice involves payment, is this sufficient for its consideration as a crime?

No. Illegal practice of medicine which aims at profit and healing practices performed for payment submit the agent[67] to a fine penalty as well, according to the sole paragraph of articles 282 and 284 of the Penal Code.

May a given punishment be more severe depending on the result of the crime?

Yes. If any of the cited crimes result in serious bodily harm the freedom privative punishment is increased by half. If they result in death the punishment is doubled. As for other health-related negligent crimes, if they result in bodily harm the punishment is increased by half; if they result in death the law applies the sentence suited for manslaughter (1 to 3 years) which is increased by a third.[68]

---

[67] Agent: individual who commits a crime.
[68] Penal Code, arts. 258 and 285.

5. Malice and negligence

What is a malice crime and a negligent crime?

A malice crime is an intentional offense whereas a negligent crime is a result of imprudence, inability, or negligence.

According to an explanation for non-specialists in Law, what is malice and negligence?

In order to understand juridical arguments it is indeed necessary for a person to understand the concepts of malice and negligence in Law, especially due to the significant difference in meaning between juridical terminology and popular knowledge. Guilt is popularly understood as an 'intention' and the common expression 'I am not guilty' equates to 'I had no intention'. In Law there is a slight difference: when there is an intention or will towards a certain objective a person acts with malice, just as malice constitutes a situation in which "one does not intend for the result to happen but even so assumes the risk of producing it". On the other hand an individual acts with guilt (negligence) when he/she causes a given result because of inability (lack of technical knowledge), imprudence (reckless action), and negligence (omission, lack of caution).

Are crimes always malicious or can they be negligent as well?

In general crimes are malicious. If they are negligent a legal prediction must be in order.

As far as crimes related to spiritual healing are concerned, is a negligent form possible?

No. Illegal practice of medicine, charlatanism, and healing are crimes which may only occur in the malicious form, in other words, if the agent wishes for a result or assumes the risk of producing it. Crimes caused by imprudence, inability, or negligence are not possible.

If no malice is declared and the accused is acquitted, does not the simple fact of being sued constitute a reason for revolt in whoever promotes spiritual healing?

It may indeed seem that a lawsuit itself equates to injustice. However individuals who serve as an instrument for good spirits in spiritual healing procedures receive this task not as a privilege but as a divine mission, which is the only way that allows them to bear misunderstandings and persecutions.

What normally happens, in other words, what injustices are suffered by mediums who serve as apparatus in spiritual healing?

Common occurrences involve police investigations and accusations in criminal lawsuits for illegal practice of medicine and healing.

6. Attempt

May a mere attempt of illegal practice of medicine, charlatanism, and healing occur?

Illegal practice of medicine does not allow for an attempt because it refers to a regular conduct. Similarly, healing is only characterized as a crime when regularity occurs and this is not possible in an attempt. However, charlatanism allows for attempts because it does constitute a regular crime.

What does 'attempted crime' mean in the Penal Code?

The Penal Code has established precise norms.

A crime may be:

I – committed, if it involves all the elements of its legal definition;

II – attempted, if it is not consummated due to circumstances which are contrary to the agent's will.[69]

7. Aiding and Abetting

May an individual who assists in criminal offenses of illegal practice of medicine, charlatanism, and healing also receive punishment?

Yes. Regardless of a crime's public or private sphere, if the agent is convicted then whoever helped him/her in a criminal offense will be regarded as an accomplice and may consequently receive punishment. This is expressed in article 29 of the Penal Code: "An individual who participates in criminal offenses in any way is liable for sentences referred to such offenses according to the degree of culpability."

---

[69] Penal Code, art. 14.

8. Public penal action

What does 'public action' mean?

Criminal offenses may refer to private action[70] or public action[71]. The latter may be conditioned to representation[72] or unconditioned[73]. As far as an unconditioned public action is concerned legal measures may be taken even against the wish of the alleged victim or his/her legal representative.

Do crimes related to spiritual healing refer to private action or public action?

Illegal practice of medicine, charlatanism, and even healing refer to unconditioned public action.

Does this mean that legal measures may be taken even if the benefited individual does not wish it?

Yes. The logic reveals that the benefited individual has no personal interest in a criminal lawsuit against the medium who acted as a mediator for spiritual healing. Nevertheless a police inquiry may be conducted and the criminal lawsuit may be initiated even against the wish of the benefited individual.

9. Criminal instruction and judgment

In a real case, how is a judge to know whether spiritual manifestation actually occurred or a fraud is involved?

As soon as a judge receives an accusation and consents to a lawsuit he/she summons the accused for a defense against the accusation that has

---

[70] When the initiative of the criminal lawsuit belongs to the alleged victim based on his/her complaint or on that of his/her legal representative.

[71] When the initiative of the lawsuit belongs to the Public Prosecution Office (public prosecutor) based on an accusation.

[72] The word 'representation' has several meanings in Law. When the law states that the initiative of the State depends on representation in order to promote an investigation (Civil Police) and to offer an accusation (Public Prosecution Office) for the start of a lawsuit, it means that the victim or its legal representative must give authorization (to consent, to allow) for legal measures to be taken.

[73] Unconditioned public action does not depend on representation.

been filed on to him/her. Defense in its amplitude is a guarantee for citizens stated in the Federal Constitution[74]. Whatever the offense processual instruction produces evidence and selects witness statements. At the end of procedures, after defense and prosecution allegations regarding the presented evidence have been made, the magistrate will state the sentence which convicts or acquits the defendant.

What does 'processual instruction' mean?

Technically the expression is 'criminal instruction', in other words, it is a phase in the lawsuit in which evidence is produced and diligences are carried out in order for all doubts related to the penal illicit case to be solved.

Is it not difficult for the magistrate to decide whether real spiritual treatment or mere trickery occurred in a given case?

Not if the instruction is effectively carried out. In order for this to happen, both the prosecution and the defense can and must provide evidence. Even so, if the judge remains in doubt at the end of instruction he/she must acquit the accused, based on the principle of *in dubio pro reo*, according to which "It is better to let nine guilty men free than to convict one innocent man".

As far as cases which involve actual fraud and/or attainment of financial gain are concerned, are offenders charged?

Yes. There are countless cons in the name of religion throughout Brazil. When a judge is convinced of criminal practice based on the body of evidence of the penal lawsuit, then the decision will consist of a conviction.

What is body of evidence?

The answer can be found in the question itself. It is a set of evidence collected during criminal instruction which allows a magistrate to judge for conviction or acquittal.

---

[74] FC, art. V: LV: "to the litigants, in a judicial or administrative process, and to the defendants in general, are assured the right to contradictory and full defense...;".

10. Anticipated judgment

If a judge is convinced of the non-existence of a crime, may he judge the lawsuit in advance?

He may not receive the accusation. However, if the accusation is received – via the current penal processual juridical system – he may only acquit the accused in the final sentence after providing the latter with the ample right of defense against the accusation at hand.

Even if the judge receives an accusation may he acquit the accused in advance, i.e. before the hearing sessions of witnesses?

There is a concept in Brazilian civil lawsuits known as *summary judgment*, which occurs when the magistrate – after the lawsuit has been judged based on the author's action and on the defense of the accused – concludes that there is no matter of fact to be proved but only a matter of law to be decided.[75] Thus a decision is announced in advance without further delay.

As far as the penal lawsuit is concerned an anticipated judgment is not permitted. Clearly the field of Law progresses to a sole decision of acquittal in the future, because conviction in advance would violate the constitutional guarantee of full defense. It is true that some magistrates already employ anticipated judgment in order to declare a perspective or virtual prescription, a prescription based on the probable sentence. However, an anticipated trial for acquittal – judgment of merit and announcement of the innocence of the defendant – is as yet not possible.

What is merit?

Merit is the actual fact, in other words, the appointed criminal conduct as stated in the Penal Code. Certain norms stated by the Code of Penal Procedure must be followed in the investigation. Once the lawsuit is concluded the judge declares the decision of merit and convicts or acquits the defendant. If the judge received an accusation he/she will only be able to declare acquittal in the sentence at the end of the action.

---

[75] CCP (Code of Civil Procedure), art. 330: "The judge will announce a sentence after direct knowledge of the petition:

I – when merit is solely a matter of law or, if it is a matter of law and of fact, there is no need to present evidence at a court session;"

Is there no other alternative?

In a given 'comarca' the medium João was charged and accused of illegal practice of medicine and healing. The accusation was received and he was summoned for questioning. During questioning he claimed that he did not know anything about the charge because he was incorporated whenever he prescribed medication or performed healing. As a medium he only acted as an instrument for spirits. After questioning the magistrate talked with the representative from the Public Prosecution Office and declared that he would conclude the lawsuit at that moment if no appeals were filed. The judge added that he had to judge various criminal lawsuits concerning homicides, theft, robbery, kidnappings, rapes, and other violent crimes, and that there was no point in the Judiciary wasting time with that particular lawsuit in which the accused party had not done anything to harm people. In fact records included only benefited individuals, not harmed ones. With the agreement of the public prosecutor and without any manifestation from the defense, the judge called the lawsuit to order and reviewed the former decision of acceptance of the accusation; he did not accept the latter and declared the dismissal of the case. The representative of the Public Prosecution Office was summoned but he did not file an appeal, and the judgment passed into matter adjudged.

11. Prescription

Once the publication of Spiritual Cures was authorized, the statements included the dates on which they were written. For what reason were these dates not included in this book?

The dates were not included in order to prevent such public information from being used judicially against the medium João. Information provided by those benefited from spiritual healing is deliberately presented in a rather vague form, without any reference to dates. The author was careful to publish only cases which may not be used to file a criminal lawsuit against the medium João for illegal practice of medicine, charlatanism, or healing due to prescription.

What is 'prescription'?

It means that the State (Judiciary) has lost the right to punish due to the time lapsed before the conclusion of the lawsuit.

Does prescription often occur in Brazil?

Yes, for various reasons, especially the excessive amount of lawsuits. The Judiciary simply cannot provide decisions for the great number of filed lawsuits.

12. Crimes of lesser offensive potential

Even if one hypothetically assumes that spiritual healing constitutes a penal offense, would it not be regarded as a less serious crime?

Yes, illegal practice of medicine, charlatanism, and even healing are crimes of lesser offensive potential.

How are offenses classified considering their serious or offensive potential?

Offenses whose maximum sentence do not exceed two years have less offensive potential[76]; if a minimum sentence is not superior to one year the offense will be considered a medium offensive potential[77]; an infraction that does not have lesser or medium offensive potential will be regarded as a higher offensive potential crime, which means that its minimal sentence is superior to one year of incarceration.

What changes in a lawsuit if an offense has lesser offensive potential?

In Criminal Procedure proceedings consist of a legal action or a set of actions of a given lawsuit. In case of infractions with lesser offensive potential legal proceedings allow for an agreement in order to prevent a lawsuit from being filed. In case of infractions with medium offensive

---

[76] According to Law n. 9.099/95, infractions whose maximum sentence did not exceed one year (art. 61) were considered of lesser offensive potential. Subsequently Law n. 11.313/06 changed this article and increased the time period to two years.

[77] Law n. 9.099/95, art. 89: "In the case of crimes whose minimum sentence is equal to or inferior to 1 (one) year, included in the present Law or not, the Public Prosecution Office responsible for filing the accusation may pose the suspension of the lawsuit for 2 (two) to 4 (years), as long as the defendant is not being sued or has not been convicted of another offense. The remaining requirements for authorization of the conditional suspension of the sentence must also be complied with (art. 77 of the Penal Code)".

potential an agreement may be used to cancel a lawsuit[78]. No form of agreement is possible in the case of infractions with higher offensive potential.

Are crimes connected with spiritual healing of lesser offensive potential?

Yes. Maximum sentences do not exceed two years because such offenses are not so serious.

13. Appeal

Can an appeal be filed after a judge's conviction or acquittal verdict?

Yes. Appeals are constitutionally guaranteed by Brazilian Law[79]. There are two instances of jurisdiction: the suitor which does not agree with the judge's decision (first instance) may file an appeal to the second instance of jurisdiction (Court of Justice). If a defendant is acquitted the prosecutor may appeal if he/she wishes. In case of conviction, the defense may also file an appeal.

Are many appeals filed in criminal lawsuits related to spiritual healing?

No. As a rule all is solved at the first instance of jurisdiction. In the author's opinion several circumstances must be considered. First of all it is a known fact that there is a great deal of prescription because of the sentences stated by law.

---

[78] FC, art. 98: "The Union, in the Federal District and Territories, and the States will establish:
I – Special courts constituted by full judges or full and lay judges which are competent in conciliation, judgment, and execution of civil causes of lower complexity as well as criminal offenses of lesser offensive potential, in accordance with oral and summary proceedings. Transaction and judgment of appeals by groups of first instance judges are permitted in accordance with the law.
Law n. 9.099/95, art. 76: "In case of representation or if an offense requires unconditioned public criminal action, which does not refer to discontinuance, the Public Prosecution Office may pose the immediate application of the sentence restrictive of rights or fines to be specified in the proposal".

[79] FC, art. 5: LV: "to the litigants, in a judicial or administrative process, and to the defendants in general, are assured the right to contradictory and full defense, with their inherent means and resources;".

There is also a widely spread belief among magistrates that crimes related to illegal practice of medicine, charlatanism, and healing constitute minor offenses and do not deserve any kind of priority treatment on the part of the Judiciary. Only those cases which involve evident frauds go to trial.

Finally, if one considers that every citizen is free to perform his/her cult publicly –only practices which offend public morality and laws are condemnable -, the magistrate is aware of the constitutional protection for religious freedom in real serious cases.

The vast majority of occurrences are solved at the first instance of jurisdiction with convictions of fraudulent cases and acquittal of serious spiritual healing cases. The number of appeals is reduced.

14. Psychography and copyright

In the case of psychographed books dictated by spirits who had families when they were incarnate, does the copyright belong to their heirs?

No. Justice states that copyright ends with death, therefore one cannot talk of copyright for heirs because spirits do not have heirs or successors.

Does the law protect copyright for an indeterminate period of time?

No. Legal protection is solely provided for intellectual production during an author's life and for a certain period of time after his/her death. Legal protection currently lasts for 70 years[80].

Are there any real episodes regarding this topic?

Yes, there is a case which involves books dictated by the spirit Humberto de Campos and psychographed by Francisco Cândido Xavier.

Who was Humberto de Campos?[81]

Humberto de Campos (1886-1934) was a renowned journalist, politician, critic, chronicler, poet, biographer, memorialist, and a member of the Brazilian Academy of Letters with an extensive intellectual production. He read the

---

[80] Law n. 9.610 from February 19, 1998, art. 41: "Patrimonial author's rights lasts for seventy years starting from January 1 of the year after his/her death in accordance with the successor order of civil law".

[81] For further reference see Chapter I, n. 2.

book *Parnaso de Além-Túmulo* – a collection of poems dictated by spirits of several disincarnate poets – and made praiseful remarks about it.[82] Despite such praise Humberto de Campos made an unusual remark: he claimed that books dictated by disincarnate spirits resulted in unfair competition, for incarnate writers such as himself had to deal with daily survival.[83]

What is the connection between Humberto de Campos and Chico Xavier?

There was no connection during Campos' life. When Campos' spirit disincarnated it dictated an extensive literary work which was psychographed by Chico Xavier and published by the Brazilian Spiritist Federation.

Messages, short stories, chronicles, novellas, and poems, in other words, all that was dictated by the spirit Humberto de Campos and psychographed by the respected medium from Minas Gerais was published (*Novas Mensagens* (New Messages); *Boa Nova* (Good News); *Reportagens de Além-Túmulo* (Reports From Beyond the Grave); *Brasil – Coração do Mundo, Pátria do Evangelho* (Brazil, Heart of the World, Nation of Gospels); and *Crônicas de Além-Túmulo* (Chronicles From Beyond the Grave). The copyright was offered by Chico Xavier to the Brazilian Spiritist Federation.

What was the intention of the family of Humberto de Campos?

The widow of Humberto de Campos filed a judicial action against the Brazilian Spiritist Federation and against Francisco Cândido Xavier with the intention of obtaining a decision by the Judiciary on whether the literary work belonged to the "spirit" of Humberto de Campos or not.

In case of a negative decision the petition requested:

a) The apprehension of all existing copies in circulation;

b) Criminal sanctions to those responsible for the publication;

c) Prohibition of the use of the name of Humberto de Campos in any literary publication;

d) Payment of losses and damages on the part of those responsible for the publication.

---

[82] Brazilian Academy of Letters. In: CAMPOS, Humberto de. Available at: http://www.biblio.com.br/templates/humbertodecampos/humbertodecampos.htm. Accessed: may 09 2005.

[83] SOUTO MAIOR, Marcel. *As Vidas de Chico Xavier*, p. 48.

In case of a positive decision the petition requested:

a) A statement on whether the copyright belonged exclusively to the family of Humberto de Campos or to the Spiritist world represented by the Brazilian Spiritist Federation, as well as a statement on whether the psychographic medium had any literary or economic participation in the publication;

b) The recognition of the rights of the family of Humberto de Campos, so the title-holders of such rights might use the works in any way they wished;

c) A decision on whether the Brazilian Spiritist Federation would be charged by legal sanctions stated by Law because of the publication of the works.[84]

Did the lawsuit attract much attention?

More than can be imagined. The press in general had already widely discussed whether Francisco Cândido Xavier's first publication (*Parnaso de Além-Túmulo*) was in fact a literary production dictated by spirits of disincarnate poets or plain myth. Renowned scholars, respected literary critics, and representatives from different religious creeds became involved in the controversy. The main polemic concerned the possibility of admitting the existence of life after death as well as communication from beyond the grave. This polemic increased considerably after the legal action filed by the family of Humberto de Campos. Many jurists joined the scholars and critics in this regard. The press dedicated special attention to the case, as often happens with stories that attract public interest.

What was the position taken up by Chico Xavier in this lawsuit?

This lawsuit deeply upset Chico Xavier due to the press repercussion and the possibility of going to jail as a trickster.

What was the decision of the Judiciary regarding such spiritual manifestations?

After brilliant pleading on the part of the lawyer representing the Brazilian Spiritist Federation and Chico Xavier (Miguel Timponi) the Judiciary judged the plaintiff's action groundless. An appeal was filed but the Court of Justice

---

[84] TIMPONI, Miguel. *A Psicografia Ante os Tribunais*, p. 12/13.

maintained the decision of the monocratic judge and ended the discussion. The precedent remained and this notorious lawsuit acted as publicity for Spiritism and made the medium Francisco Cândido Xavier even more famous.

Were other books dictated by the spirit of Humberto de Campos subsequently?

Yes, but since then the works psychographed by Chico Xavier and dictated by the spirit Humberto de Campos have been identified as dictations by the spirit of "Brother X".

15. Psychography as judicial proof

Does the Brazilian penal juridical system accept psychographed messages as evidence?

It must be stated that there are crimes whose judgment is provided by a single judge (Court judge) and crimes judged by a Court of Jury (juries). The Constitution states that a Court of Jury is responsible for malice offenses (intentional) against life, both consummated or attempted: homicide; inducement, instigation, or aid in suicide; infanticide; and abortion[85]. Members of the jury detain the sovereignty of their verdicts[86] and therefore may accept psychographed messages as evidence. As for the crimes to be judged by a single judge, the latter must form a decision according to his/her own conviction[87]. In order to do so, the judge analyzes the body of evidence and may also take phychographed messages into account.

The Spiritist literature makes reference to the so-called "Case of Goiânia". What was this case like?

A homicide which occurred in Goiânia, the capital city of Goiás State, received great attention from the national and international press because the magistrate (Orimar de Bastos) also based his decision on letters which had

---

[85] CCP, art. 74, § 1.

[86] FC, art. 5, XXXVIII: "the institution of the jury is recognized with the organization provided by the law and the following must be assured:
a) fullness of defense;
b) secrecy in voting;
c) sovereignty of the verdicts;
d) competence for the judgment of malicious crimes against life;"

[87] CCP, art. 157: "The judge will form his/her conviction on free appreciation of evidence".

been psychographed by Chico Xavier. Two young men had been playing with a gun after having unloaded it. This episode took place at the house of the defendant (José Divino Nunes) and the gun belonged to his father (accused). Maurício Garcez Henrique, the young man who had removed the bullets, was shot by his friend who was unaware that the gun still contained one bullet. The young man who fired the gun was charged, accused, and sued for murder. There were no witnesses. The victim stated his friend's innocence in several psychographed letters to his parents and declared that it had been an accident and that his friend was not to blame. The victim's parents compared his signature on his identity card with that on the psychographed letter and considered them identical. The letters also included names of some of the victim's relatives which were unknown to the medium.

At first, the magistrate analyzed the aspect concerning 'intention' and concluded that a malice offense had not occurred. After that he analyzed the hypothesis of 'negligence' and concluded that the accused could not be found guilty either because of the unpredictability of the episode.

The Brazilian Law declares that homicide offenses are to be judged by a Court of Jury. There is an initial phase under the responsibility of the Law Judge, and the latter declares one of the following decisions after evidence is gathered: a) indicment: refers the accused to trial by the Court of Jury; b) acquittal: stops the lawsuit due to lack of factual evidence or authorial evidence; c) acquits the defendant: the judge admits an undeniable cause which is crime-excluding, such as self-defense; d) declassifies the offense: the judge concludes that the offense at hand is not to be judged by the Court of Jury, for instance in an accusation of murder, in which the magistrate may conclude that bodily harm was followed by death and thus the competence for judgment belongs to the judge, not to the Jury.

As far as the present case is concerned, the magistrate considered the accusation groundless because the committed offense was of an unpredictable nature and therefore did not relate to any of the sanctions stated by the Brazilian Penal Code. In addition to the *ex officio* appeal – according to which the magistrate himself submits his decision to appreciation by the Court of Justice – the Public Prosecution Office filed an appeal against the acquittal. The Court of Justice referred the defendant to trial by the Court of Jury. A new appeal by the Public Prosecution Office was denied and acquittal was sustained.[88]

---

[88] Hércio Marcos C. Arantes. *Lealdade*, p. 11/28, 37/41, 78/79, and 91/94. In addition to consultation of various publications, the author personally interviewed judge Orimar de Bastos who stated the verdict of acquittal.

A letter which had been psychographed by Chico Xavier and dictated by the spirit Alencar Furtado Filho allegedly influenced the final decision. What actually happened?

In 1982, the political panorama in Brazil was tense due to the slow political opening which eventually resulted in the transfer of power from the military to civilians. One of the political leaders at the time was the politician Alencar Furtado, whose term of office was banned by the "Revolution". In such a heavily charged political environment, the 26-year-old federal deputy Heitor Alencar Furtado Filho was murdered when he returned home from a political rally. He parked the car at the side of the road in order to rest and was approached by a policeman (José Aparecido Branco) who fired a shot at him. The policeman claimed the shot had been accidental but the political context of the period induced the conclusion that the victim had been executed on someone's orders. Political manifestations and exposure in the press indicated that the trial would end with a conviction for qualified murder.

Chico Xavier psychographed a message dictated by the victim which stated that the shot had been "accidental". The victim's father examined the message and admitted that it indeed belonged to his son. The initial prediction of 30 years of incarceration was reduced to 8 years and 20 days.

Are there similar lawsuits in which the spiritual communication of a homicide victim influenced a trial?

Yes. In the 1980s Gleide Dutra de Deus, former Miss Campo Grande (present capital of the state of Mato Grosso do Sul), was shot in the neck and her husband João Francisco de Deus was accused of the crime. All components typical of passionate crimes were present: the victim had been a beautiful woman and her husband an extremely jealous man who used to carry a gun with him. The defendant's claim of an accidental shot was weak because the victim, just before her death, had told two nurses at the hospital that her husband was not to blame for the shot.

The defendant sought spiritual support from Chico Xavier. Gleide dictated a message to Chico and expressed her husband's innocence. The Court of Jury acquitted the defendant by seven votes to zero in the first trial. In the second trail the defendant was convicted of manslaughter and sentenced to one year of incarceration, but he was not arrested because prescription had already ourred.[89]

---

[89] CANAL JUSTIÇA. http://www.canaljustiça.jor.br/index.php?id=15628. Accessed: sep 12 2005.

16. Zé Arigó

Was Zé Arigó, the renowned medium from Minas Gerais, criminally sued?

Yes, but spiritual healing was not classified as a crime of lesser offensive potential at the time.

Who was Zé Arigó?

José Pedro de Freitas, known as "Zé Arigó", was born in Congonhas do Campo, Minas Gerais State, in 1921.[90] By incorporating the spirit of Dr. Fritz,[91] Zé Arigó performed scientifically unexplainable surgeries and was internationally famous for surgeries without anesthesia or any kind of asepsis and which employed rudimentary instruments (scissors, spoons, knives, and rusty penknives).[92] He became famous during the 1950s and 1960s, despite having offered services in Congonhas before this time. Political involvement and excessive media publicity exposed Zé Arigó to criminal lawsuits.

What was the criminal lawsuit against Zé Arigó like?

He was criminally sued twice for healing and illegal practice of medicine. The first lawsuit began in 1956 and resulted in a conviction of 1 year and 3 months of incarceration. An appeal reduced this sentence to eight months in prison. Before he was arrested he was reprieved by the President Juscelino Kubitschek.[93] Zé Arigó was once again sued and convicted to 1 year and 4 months of imprisonment. He remained in jail for some time in 1962 in the town of Conselheiro Lafaiete, Minas Gerais, a neighboring town of Congonhas do Campo. Zé Arigó was a victim of a work accident and died on January 11, 1971.[94]

[90] BASÍLIO, José. José Pedro de Freitas (Zé Arigó). Available at: http://www.geae.inf.br/pt/biografias/arigo.php. Accessed: jan 11 2005.

[91] Dr. Fritz was a German doctor who died during the Second World War.

[92] FULLER, John G. *ARIGÓ*: O Cirurgião da Faca Enferrujada, p. 6/10.

[93] It must be mentioned that Juscelino Kubitschek was a doctor and one of his daughters was healed by the medium Zé Arigó.

[94] FULLER, John G. *ARIGÓ*: O Cirurgião da Faca Enferrujada, p. 21/25, 130/133, 137, 152/171, 224/229.

17. Criminally-sued famous mediums

In addition to the previous cases, were there other lawsuits against famous mediums?

Yes, several, among which are the following:

Inácio Bittencourt

Inácio Bittencourt was born in Portugal on April 19, 1862 and died in Rio de Janeiro on February 18, 1943. He was a prescribing medium and a healer and was criminally sued on several occasions on the charge of illegal practice of medicine. Nevertheless he was always acquitted; for instance, a historical decision was declared by the Supreme Federal Court on October 27, 1943 which admitted the existence of spiritual manifestation to be protected by the Constitution.[95]

Eurípedes Barsanulfo[96]

Eurípedes Barsanulfo is highly important for Brazilian Spiritism. He was sued in 1917 due to illegal practice of medicine. The lawsuit was discontinued due to prescription because judges did not wish to take up the case.[97]

Domingos Filgueiras

In 1904 the medium from Rio de Janeiro Domingos Filgueiras and the then president of the Brazilian Spiritist Federation were sued under the charge of healing because of the death of a woman who had smallpox and was medicated by the medium. The action was considered groundless in relation to both defendants because there was no evidence in the lawsuit records that linked the victim's death with the apprehended medication.

Filgueiras was a prescribing and healing medium and he suffered several lawsuits, the last in 1905. Successive cures obtained by his mediumistic prescriptions troubled the medical category. Public Health Inspection turned against him but his reputation remained intact after all accusations of illegal practice of medicine and he was always acquitted.[98]

---

[95] BITTENCOURT, Inácio. Available at: http://www.omensageiro.com.br/personalidades/personalidade-8.htm. Accessed: sep 12 2005.

[96] For further references see Chapter IV, n. 6.

[97] BARSANULFO, Eurípedes. Available at: http://www.terraespiritual.locaweb.com.br/Espiritismo/biografia53.html. Accessed: sep 12 2005.

[98] FILGUEIRAS, Domingos. Available at: http://www.universoespirita.org.br/textos-voluntários/DOMINGOS.htm. Accessed: sep 13 2005.

18. Doctrinal opinions

Are there favorable attitudes under the doctrinal aspect concerning spiritual healing?

Yes. Several authors express highly favorable comments on spiritual healing and always attempt to distinguish between frauds and scientifically unexplainable occurrences.

Even though comments hereby presented refer to Brazilian Law, are there authors in foreign doctrines who express a favorable attitude toward spiritual healing?

Lessons by the well-known jurist Jimenez de Asúa are hereby opportune for their juridical relevance; Asúa believes that there is no penal responsibility whenever mental disorder occurs, albeit momentary. If this occurs the transitory privation of conscience constitutes an excluding cause of criminality, in other words:

> First of all, a mental disturbance of immediate, evidenced, and transitory cause which ends in cure and is different from permanent disturbance; secondly, a proved pathological basis; thirdly, which produces annulment of free will and generally of conscience, and mere obfuscation is not sufficient. (ASÚA, 1942, p. 265)

Other quotations are equally important and are presented below:

> That is the reason why the English joyfully designate its state in the course of such functions as trance, which indicates a passage to another state of being, as if they wished to declare that they are unconscious in such conditions... irresponsible. (IMBASSAHY, p. 85)

> The adviser Aksakof guarantees in his classic work *Animism and Spiritism*: "All spirits know that their manifestations do not depend on the medium's will, be they intellectual or physical manifestations; the medium is incapable of promoting them. (AKSAKOF *apud* IMBASSAHY, p. 92)

> We must also remember that a medium does not possess a more comprehensive understanding of the phenomenon than the experimenter; on the contrary, he may understand even less because he is not aware of what goes on while in a trance... Whatever the source of manifest intelligence it would be completely beyond normal human faculties... All we

can say is that there is an occult intelligence, an extraordinary affirmation, behind such manifestations which destroys all known foundations of materialism. (BARRET *apud* IMBASSAHY, p. 97)

It is fair to fight suspicious healers who trick the public for profit. However, to persecute completely disinterested individuals whose sole joy consists in relieving the suffering of others is a revolting injustice. (FERRIÈRE *apud* IMBASSAHY, p. 249)

Specifically which remarks made by Brazilian doctrinaires on spiritual healing may be quoted?

Several, as follows:

People who perform healing through methods which make up a ritual of the religion they embrace are not active offenders. (JESUS, Damásio)

A medium does not act by himself. There is an extrinsic force which produces phenomena. All metapsychist authors, even those who are contrary to the intervention of the dead, emphasize this peculiarity: a medium in trance often reveals an entirely different personality; he acts under a strange influence and is not always capable of freeing himself from it.

Therefore it is not possible to guarantee that a healing medium or a prescribing medium is aware of his act and may always act freely. (IMBASSAHY, p. 81)

Mediumship involves partial or total interruption of the conscious activity of the medium in trance. (IMBASSAHY, p. 82)

What about religious rituals in which surgical procedures are performed in order to overcome the evils that afflict a victim by bodily perforations, amputations etc, do they consist of crimes? An ignorant individual who does not possess any kind of medical knowledge cannot answer for the crime of healing because such an action cannot be linked to a typical penal figure. By analyzing the incise II we can see that the article makes references to the use of gestures, words, or of any other means. A surgical procedure cannot be included in the generic formula "any other means" simply because it does not resemble the use of gestures and words, which prevents an analogical integration. Such a procedure cannot answer for the crime of illegal practice of medicine either because this offense requires the agent to possess medical knowledge but not professional authorization. The offender will answer for the crime of bodily harm. However, if an individual does possess medical knowledge, the offense of illegal practice of medicine may occur. (CAPEZ, p. 244)

Strong indication of malice must always be investigated in order to identify the offense of charlatanism. Furthermore, there must a concern towards verifying whether a fact occurs with unmistakable malice on the part of the agent. (BITENCOURT, p. 269)

It is imperative that healing be adopted as a means or as one of the means of life. (BENTO DE FARIA *apud* IMBASSAHY, p. 77)

19. Judicial decisions

As far as jurisprudence is concerned, are there judicial decisions that were favorable to accused individuals of spiritual healing?

Yes. A few decisions are presented below:

The position of hands and gestures made in the style of passes which have a strictly religious basis and aim for cures of a spiritual nature are not included in the criminal offense known as healing. Art. 284, II, of the Penal Code, in accordance with its stated terms, may include the subject of faith, but respective practices must be assessed by morality, good customs, and public order. (RF, 184/333)

Strong indication of malice must always be investigated in order to identify the offense of charlatanism. Furthermore, there must a constant concern towards verifying whether a fact occurs with unmistakable malice on the part of the agent. (RT, 299/434)

In the act of healing, in any of its modalities, the existence of malice is presupposed, i.e. the agent wishes a given result or assumes the risk of producing it, which cannot happen with the mediumistic individual. The latter, under a state of 'trance', finds himself unconscious and therefore may not be held responsible for the actions of spirits incorporated by him. (RT, 304/498)

'Passes' constitute a common practice in the Spiritist religion and do not refer to the offense of healing because it also exists in other religions under various names. (RT, 404/282)

Passes are a part of rituals in Spiritism, similarly to blessings given by Catholic priests, and thus do not refer to the offense stated in art. 284. (RT, 404/282)

Non-characterized offense. Defendant announces healing of maladies through gestures and words. Healing was performed through natural water. Good faith was thus characterized. Unawareness of illicitness of conduct. Acquittal. Subjective element of offense of art. 284 of the Penal Code was absent and essential malice was not proved. Therefore configuration of offense was not verified. (RT, 425/328)

The good faith of a person who believes to be a "mediumistic apparatus" may remove the aspect of malice. (RT, 425/328)

If healing advocated by the defendant for the cure of people's maladies was sought by a group through prayers – a question of pure faith –, such practice does not refer to healing due to the freedom of cult assured by the Constitution. (RT, 446/414)

The offense of healing is not characterized if the defendants, representatives of religious sects, only resorted to prayer and to taking care of the health of those who sought them for the cure of their illnesses. (RT 452/406)

Crime against public health. Healing. Decharacterization – Missionary of a registered sect which announces miraculous cures in its religious practices through a sick person's faith in God, by the ointment of water and blessed oils and distribution of hosts – Lack of evidence that the missionary diagnosed, prescribed medication, or offered potions to sick individuals which might have been regarded as miraculous or impregnated by secret and supernatural qualities – practices thus common in other religions – Acquittal was declared – Application of art. 386, VI, of CCP and intelligence of art. 284 of PC. (TACrimSP - RT, 642/314)

Charlatanism and Healing. Offenses attributed to leader of religious sect. Accusation fails to state whether attributed conducts might have produced the probability of damage. Ineptitude was declared. Freedom of cult is assured by the Constitution. Absence of just cause for penal action. Suspension of action was stated. Habeas Corpus was given. (RT, 699/376)

I cannot consider healing by supernatural means as medical practice. The appellant does not prescribe, he states that he invokes spirits and these in fact prescribe. Thus this is a practice of a given cult. I do not regard the appellant's proceeding as medical practice but as manifestation of a religious belief which deserved to be accepted like any other religious belief... I have never witnessed anyone's attempt to sue ecclesiastical authorities in charge of churches that perform miracles. Healing performed in Spiritism means believing in the intervention of spirits, just as we Catholics believe in supernatural intervention. For these reasons the fact may be regarded as a manifestation of belief, not as medical practice. (IMBASSAHY, p. 122)

The medium who is incorporated by a spirit or by a strange force is unable to predict any kind of result; and even if he sits calmly at a small table and waits for the 'force' to come and prescribe medication, the result the medium expects is good, what he supposes is always a good result. The prediction of a good result does not constitute an element of the offense. (IMBASSAHY, p. 124)

When all the prescribed and inspected medications are products exclusively based on vitamins, are not narcotic substances or lead to physical or psychic dependence, are not harmful to a person's health or cause side effects, and may be sold without medical prescription, then a healing offense is not in order. (FRANCO, 1987, p. 1010)

The act of blessing which is commonplace in many religions and creeds is performed throughout the country; if those who perform blessing do not use it as a means to earn a living, then a healing offense is not in order. (FRANCO, 1987, p. 1013)

HC – Penal – Penal Lawsuit – Freedom of cult – Charlatanism – Healing – Accusation – Ineptitude. An accusation must describe the criminal offense in all its circumstances in order to allow the right of defense. Charlatanism and healing are included in the list of crimes against public health, in other words, crimes which are committed against an indeterminate number of people. Crimes of concrete danger (probability of damage). The Penal Law of negligence is incompatible with abstract danger, a mere hypothesis. An individual must be held responsible for what he did or did not do. Simple supposition must be refuted. Therefore an accusation must present the result (normative sense), otherwise it will be inept. Freedom of cult is a constitutional guarantee, which also offers protection for the place of liturgy. (STJ, HC n. 1.498)

The Author

Who is the author?

The author is a university professor and one of the lawyers of the medium João and of Casa de Dom Inácio.

Which public offices has the author occupied?

Registrar, expert, police chief, and public prosecutor.

Apart from these public offices, has the author occupied other posts?

Yes, he is a former Dean of the Law School at Universidade Católica de Goiás and President of Ordem dos Advogados do Brasil ("Order of Brazilian Lawyers") in the state of Goiás.

What is the author's religion?

The author does not have a specific religion. He declares himself a "Catholic-Spiritist", if such duplicity of religions is possible. Nevertheless, he regards all religions with deep respect.

Would not the author be a Catholic and only a Spiritist sympathizer?

No. He is a sympathizer of several religions, but in relation to Spiritism his regard goes beyond that. The author is comfortable in stating that he is an adept of Catholicism and Spiritism. In addition, he has deep family ties with the latter on both maternal and paternal sides.

The author's father (Augusto Estulano Garcia) was a Spiritist. His paternal grandfather (João Estulano Garcia) moved definitively from São Paulo to the backwoods of Goiás together with his wife (Ana Custódia de Jesus) and children, among them the author's father who was still single at the time. João Estulano acquired a rural property in the municipality of Pouso Alto (present-day Piracanjuba) and donated two "alqueires" (~ 4.84 hectares) of land for the construction of houses and the installation of a Spiritist community named "Estulânia", which still stands.

The author's mother was a medium and a worshipper of Spiritism. Her parents (Alfredo Peixoto dos Santos and Margarida Pires dos Santos) were also linked with this religion.

Is it not contradictory to consider oneself Catholic and Spiritist at the same time, to be linked with two different religions?

Religion is a human organization. However religiosity, even without any relation to a specific religion, is a much deeper sentiment that translates a belief in something which science cannot explain. There is no contradiction in having a good relationship with more than one religion, in the author's opinion. He is a Catholic because of his continuing familiarity and proximity to other Catholics, especially with directors of the institution he has worked in for more than 30 years (Universidade Católica de Goiás). At the same time he is a Spiritist due to his past family ties and to the reading of several books which focus on spiritual subjects.

Both Catholicism and Spiritism are religions, so would not one of them be sufficient?

Yes, for someone who aims solely for the religious aspect. Spiritism is not only a religion, it is a doctrine compatible with all spiritualist religions. The wondrous marvel of this doctrine's scientific and philosophical aspects is worth noticing. Spiritism killed death because it considers the latter not as the end of life, but as simply the transposition to another dimension.

How did the author first come into contact with Casa de Dom Inácio?

It is common for people to go looking for Casa de Dom Inácio moved by "pain" when, in a desperate act, they seek some form of spiritual help for the evils of body and soul; they may be moved by "love", whenever they feel the need to visit a spiritualist environment, or they may be moved by "curiosity" in an attempt to understand what happens there. In the author's particular case, his first contact with Casa de Dom Inácio was not promoted by pain, love, or even less by curiosity.

The author had already defended, as a lawyer in a criminal lawsuit, a person accused of charlatanism due to spiritual healing. He faced difficulties because neither doctrine nor jurisprudence often approach the subject. On one occasion he heard a fellow professor of Penal Law (Expedito Miranda e Silva) state that a Spiritist medium would not perform illegal practice of medicine if he used knives and penknives because of the fact that no School of Medicine teaches students to perform surgeries with such instruments and without anesthesia or asepsis. The author considered this an interesting thesis and discussed it with his colleague. Some time afterwards the latter asked whether the author could help in the defense of the medium João, who had once again been accused of illegal practice of medicine and of healing. The author accepted the proposal and began to examine the criminal records. Afterwards he was introduced to the medium João and to Casa de Dom Inácio and has never stopped attending the latter ever since.

Did the author have any health problems when he went to the Casa for the first time?

Yes, the author had serious health problems at the time of his initial contact with Casa de Dom Inácio. However, it must be stated that it was not the illness that prompted his first visit there, as he had been undergoing an alternative medical treatment at the time and expressed real hopes of a positive outcome. Nowadays the author may state without fear that knowing the Casa changed his life completely.

How did the author's "doubt" turn into a "belief" in what he witnessed there?

In a natural way. The Entity often called the author – who sat in concentration among the many assistant mediums – to witness a given spiritual surgery. Beside the incorporated medium João the author witnessed incredible scenes. He prefers not to report them because of their large number.

Common sense presents the idea that reports of several real stories by a single person do not have such credibility as individual reports of several people, each one approaching his/her personal problem.

At which specific moment did "doubt" convert to "belief"?

The author is not able to specify when this occurred. It did not take place all of a sudden but gradually, after having witnessed several facts. Whenever he was called to witness a spiritual surgery he remained vigilant in order to detect any frauds. He often observed mentally: "I am not dreaming, I am not hypnotized, nor drugged, nor drunk. I am in my natural state and alert. Is what I am witnessing true?"

Was the author ever asked by the Entity whether he believed in what he saw?

Yes. At the beginning of his participation in the procedures at Casa de Dom Inácio, after witnessing a surgery which consisted of scraping of a person's eye with the aid of a small kitchen knife and without anesthesia and asepsis, the Entity questioned him: "What is necessary for the son to believe? To witness a hundred cases of spiritual cures?" The answer was as follows: "I am sincere. I am observing everything with great attention and drawing my own conclusions".

Did the Entity know when the author started to believe?

Yes. One day, after witnessing dozens of spiritual cures and having been called by the Entity to conduct the closing of procedures, the latter remarked about the author with another designated person: "The son has indeed changed. He is a new person now".

Is it possible that the author's continuing link with the Casa might result in fanaticism?

The author has indeed dedicated considerable time to the Casa and he intends to continue doing so. There is no danger of fanaticism considering the fact that he observes everything with a rational point of view. Fanaticism escapes logic and common sense. Rational dedication to a given religion is salutary but fanatical dedication is morbid. In short, rational faith is positive and blind faith is negative.

The author participates, observes, and draws his own conclusions without any interference from others.

Are there judicial matters involving the medium João and Casa de Dom Inácio?

Yes, several. The author is only one of the lawyers representing the medium João and the Casa.

Is the author a writer?

He has other published books on Law, which is his area of professional expertise. However, this subject is radically different. He does not regard himself as a writer and, within his own limitations, has attempted to write in the simplest possible way.

REFERENCES

A VIDA DE SÃO FRANCISCO XAVIER. Available at: <http://apostolado. sites.uol.com.br/morxa.htm>. Accessed: jan 11 2005.

_____. Availabe at: <http://apostolado.sites.uol.com.br/besa.htm>. Accessed: jan 11 2005.

ADOLFO BEZERRA DE MENEZES CAVALCANTI. Available at: <http:// www.feparana.com.br/biografias/adolfo-bezerra.htm>. Accessed: jan 11 2005.

ALVES, Carlos Joel Castro. *O Espinho e a Rosa*. Uberaba: Editora Vitória, 1997.

_____. *Uma Missão de Amor*. Uberaba: Editora Vitória, 1995.

ARANTES, Hércio Marcos C. *Lealdade*. 5. ed. São Paulo: Instituto de Difusão Espírita, 1992.

AS MINAS DO REI SALOMÃO. Available at: <http://www.acasicos.com.br/ html/salomao.htm>. Accessed: jan 11 2005.

ASÚA, Jimenes de. El Criminalista: Editora La Ley, vol. 2, Buenos Aires, 1942, p. 265, *apud*. POVOA, Liberato. In: *João de Deus* – Fenômeno de Abadiânia, p. 21/22.

BARSANULFO, Euripedes. <http://www.ceismael.com.br/bio/bio08.htm>. Accessed: jan 11 2005.

_____. Available at: <http://www.terraespiritual.locaweb.com.br/Espiritismo/biografia53.html>. Accessed: sep 12 2005.

BASÍLIO, José. *Bezerra de Menezes*. Available at: <http://www.geae.inf.br/ pt/briografias/bezerra-menezes.php>. Accessed: jan 11 2005.

_____. *Zé Arigó*. Available at: <www.geae.inf.br/pt/biografias/ arigo.php>. Accessed: jan 11 2005.

BATISTA, Eva Patrícia. *Bezerra de Menezes*. Available at: <http:// www.espirito.org.br/portal/artigos/neurj/bezerra.html>. Accessed: jan 14 2005.

BERNARDO, Carlos A. *Iglesia*. Available at: <http://www.geae.inf.br/pt/ biografias/ andre-luiz.php>. Accessed: jan 14 2005.

BITENCOURT, Cezar Roberto. *Tratado de Direito Penal*. São Paulo: Saraiva, 2004, v. 4, p. 269.

BITENCOURT, Inácio. Available at: <http://www.omensageiro.com.br/ personalidade/personalidade-8.htm>. Accessed: sep 12 2005.

BRAGDON, Emma (PhD) *et al. Spiritual Alliances. 5.* ed. Woodstock (EUA): Lightening Up Press, 2004.

BRASIL. *Código de Processo Civil*. Atualizado até 10-01-2005. 35. ed. São Paulo: Saraiva, 2005.

BRASIL. *Código de Processo Penal* – Código Universitário Saraiva. Atualizado até 13-01-2005. São Paulo: Saraiva, 2005.

BRASIL. *Código Penal* – Código Universitário Saraiva. Atualizado até 13-01-2005. São Paulo: Saraiva, 2005.

BRASIL. *Constituição Federal* – Código Universitário Saraiva. Atualizado até 13-01-2005. São Paulo: Saraiva, 2005.

BRASIL. Superior Tribunal de Justiça, HC n. 1.498 – Rel. Min. Luiz Vicente Chernicchiaro.

BRASIL. Supremo Tribunal Federal. CASTRO, Ministro Viveiros de. In: IMBASSAY, Carlos. *Mediunidade e a Lei*, p. 122.

BRASILEIRO, Emídio Silva Falcão. *O Livro dos Evangelhos*. São Paulo: Lúmen Editorial, 2000.

CAMPOS, Humberto de. *Academia Brasileira de Letras*. Availabe at: <http://www.biblio.com.br/Templates/humbertodecampos/humberto decampos.htm>. Accessed: may 09 2005.

_____.Available at: <http://www.feparana.com.br/biografias/ humberto_campos.htm>. Accessed: may 09 2005.

CAPELLI, Esse. *Crestomatia Espiritualista* – A grande análise. 2. ed. Goiânia: Proluz, 2004.

_____. *Mediunidade* – Elucidações práticas. Goiânia: Proluz, 2000.

_____. *Reencarnação, a mediunidade e a BÍBLIA*. Goiânia: Proluz, 2001.

CAPEZ, Fernando. *Curso de Direito Penal* – Parte Especial. São Paulo: Saraiva, 2004, v. 3, p. 244.

DIÁRIO DA MANHÃ. Goiânia, domingo, September 11, 2005, caderno *Cidades*, p. 4.

EGITO, Lárcio do. *Grandes Iluminados* – Salomão. Availabe at: <http://joselarciodoegito.com.br/site-salomão-232htm>. Accessed: jan 11 2005.

EMMANUEL. Available at: <http:// www.ame.org.br/emmanuel.htm>. Accessed: jan 11 2005.

_____. Available at: <http://www.editoraideal.com.br/benfeitores/ benfeitores-08.htm>. Accessed: jan 14 2005.

FERAUDY, Roger. *A Terra das Araras Vermelhas*. 4. ed. Limeira: Editora do Conhecimento, 2003.

FERREIRA, Lana Basílio. *A Paranormalidade em Face da Lei e da Ciência*. Dissertação de Pós-Graduação. Recife: Faculdade de Direito – UFP, 1993.

FILGUEIRAS, Domingos. Availabe at: <http://www.universoespirita.org.br/ textos_voluntários/DOMINGOS.htm>. Accessed: sep 13 2005.

FRANCO, Alberto Silva. *et. al.* Código Penal e sua Interpretação Jurisprudencial. 2. ed., *Revista dos Tribunais*. São Paulo, 1987, p. 1010/1013.

FRANCO, Divaldo P. *No Limiar do Infinito*. 4. ed. Salvador: Livraria Espírita Alvorada – Editora, 1995.

FULLER, Jonh. *ARIGÓ:* O Cirurgião da Faca Enferrujada. São Paulo: Nova Época Editorial Ltda, 1974.

GARCIA, Ismar Estulano. *Procedimento nas Infrações de Menor Potencial Ofensivo*. Goiânia: AB Editora, 2005.

HAWKING, Stephen *et al*. *A Briefer History of Time*. Rio de Janeiro: Ediouro, 2005, p. 4, 51 e 53.

HOLTZ, Alberto. *Sapiens* – 100% Ciência, Família Super. Editora Abril, Edição 01, setembro/2004, p. 30.

HOUAISS, Antônio. *Dicionário Houaiss da língua portuguesa.* Rio de Janeiro: Editora Objetiva, 2004.

IMBASSAHY, Carlos. *A Mediunidade e a Lei.* 3. ed. Rio de Janeiro: Federação Espírita Brasileira, 1983, p. 81/82/85.

IRMÃ SCHEILLA. Availabe at: <http://www.grupoirmascheilla.com.br/ Quem%20e 20%Irma%Scheilla.htm>. Accessed: sep 15 2005.

JESUS, Damásio Evangelista de. *Direito Penal.* 15. ed. São Paulo: Saraiva, 2002, v. 3.

_____. *Direito Penal Anotado.* São Paulo: Saraiva, 1989.

KARDEC, Allan. *O Céu e o Inferno.* 52. ed. Rio de Janeiro: Federação Espírita Brasileira, 2003.

_____. *O Livro dos Espíritos.* 74. ed. Araras: Instituto de Difusão Espírita, 1992.

_____. *O Livro dos Médiuns.* 20 ed. Araras: Instituto de Difusão Espírita, 1991.

_____.*The Spirit's Book.* 10 ed. São Paulo: LAKE – Livraria Allan Kardec Editora. Tr. Anna Blackwell.

KENDALL, Margareth. *Religiões em Diálogo* – Coleção Cultura Religiosa. São Paulo: Edições São Paulo, 1997.

LEYMARIE, Madame P. C. *Processo dos Espíritos.* (Resumo em português de *Procés des Spirites*, por Hermínio C. Miranda). 2. ed. Rio de Janeiro: Federação Espírita Brasileira, 1977.

LIMA, Luiz Rocha. *Medicina dos Espíritos.* Rio de Janeiro: Educandário Social Lar de Frei Luiz, 1984.

LOPES, Jair Leonardo. *Em Defesa de Arigó.* Belo Horizonte: [s.n.], 1965.

LOYOLA, Inácio de. Available at: <http://www.fca.org.br/inacio.htm>. Accessed: jan 11 2005.

LOYOLA, Santo Inácio de. Availabe at: <http://planeta.terra.com.br/arte/sfv/StInacio.html>. Accessed: jan 11, 2005.

LUCCA, José Carlos de. *Justiça Além da Vida*. São Paulo: Petit Editora, 2004.

LUIZ, André. *Perfil e Obra*. Availabe at: <http://www.gcocities.com/Paris/Tower/1120/andre.html>. Accessed: jan 14 2005.

MAES, Hercílio. *Mediunidade de Cura*. 11 ed. Limeira: Editora Conhecimento, 2003.

MILLER, René Fülöp. *Os Santos Que Abalaram o Mundo*. Tradução de: Oscar Mendes. 16. ed. Rio de Janeiro: José Olímpio, 2004.

MORSCH, Arthur Rocha (SJ). *Inácio de Loyola*. São Paulo: Edições Loyola, 1993.

MURPHY, Joseph. *O Poder do Subconsciente*. 38. ed. Rio de Janeiro: Record, 1994.

OLIVEIRA, Weimar Muniz. *O Apóstolo do Século XX* – Chico Xavier. Goiânia: Federação Espírita do Estado de Goiás, 2001.

_____. *A Filosofia do Direito* – Além da 3ª Dimensão. 3. ed. Goiânia: Federação Espírita do Estado de Goiás, 2004.

ORTIZ, Fernando. *Filosofia Penal dos Espíritas*. 2. ed. São Paulo: LAKE – Livraria Allan Kardec Editora. Tradução de: Carlos Imbassay, 1998.

PARANHOS, Roger Bottini. *Akhenaton* – A Revolução Espiritual do Antigo Egito. Limeira: Conhecimento, 2004.

PELEGRINO-ESTRICH, Robert. *João de Deus:* O Curador e Seus Milagres. São Paulo: Editora e Gráfica Terra.

PEREIRA, Yvone. A. *Memórias de um suicida*. 2. ed. Rio de Janeiro: Federação Espírita Brasileira, 2004.

PIRES, J. Herculano. *ARIGÓ* – Vida, Mediunidade e Martírio. 4. ed. São Paulo: EME, 1998.

POVOA, Liberato. *João de Deus* – Fenômeno de Abadiânia. 5. ed. Anápolis: Editora Múltipla, 2003.

211

REVISTA "ISTO É". Cajamar: Editora Três, n. 1889, 2005.

REVISTA CRISTÃ DE ESPIRITISMO. São Paulo: Editora Vivência, ano VII, n. 37, 2005.

REVISTA ESPIRITA ALLAN KARDEC. Goiânia: ano XIII, n° 53, julho, 2005.

REVISTA PARAPSICOLOGIA. São Paulo: Editora Arte Antiga, ano 2, n. 23, 2005.

REVISTA UNIVERSO ESPÍRITA, São Paulo: Editora Universo Espírita, ano 2, n. 24/26. 2005.

REVISTA VIDA & RELIGIÃO, São Paulo: Editora ON Line, ano 1, ed. 06, 2006.

ROCHA, Osvaldo Pereira. *Rei Salomão*. Available at: <http://www.oprocha.elo.com.br /rei-salomão.htm>. Accessed: jan 12 2005.

ROHDEN, Huberto. *Setas na Encruzilhada*. Rio de Janeiro: Freitas Bastos S/A, 1967.

SAVARIS, Alfredina Arlete. *Curas Espirituais Realizadas por João Teixeira de Faria*. Monografia (Especialista em Estudos da Consciência) – Faculdade de Ciências Biopsíquicas do Paraná, Curitiba, 1997.

SCHRITZMEYER, Ana Lúcia Pastore. *Sortilégio de Saberes*: curandeiros e juizes nos tribunais brasileiros (1900 - 1990). São Paulo: IBCCRIM, 2004.

SILVA, Fernando Correia da. *Osvaldo Cruz*. Available at: <http://www.vidaslusofanas.pt/osvaldo_cruz.atm>. Accessed: jul 14 2005.

SOUTO MAIOR, Marcel. *As Vidas de Chico Xavier*. 2. ed. São Paulo: Planeta, 2003.

TELES, Ney Moura. *Direito Penal* – Parte Especial. São Paulo: Editora Atlas, 2004. v. III.

TIMPONI, Miguel. *A Psicografia Ante os Tribunais*. 5. ed. Rio de Janeiro: Federação Espírita Brasileira, 1978.

TRIBUNAL de Alçada Criminal de São Paulo. *Revista dos Tribunais*. n. 642, p. 314.

XAVIER, Chico. *Fragmentos de uma vida.* Available at: <http://www.mensageiros.org.br>. Accessed: jul 14 2005.

_____. Available at: <http://www.canaljustiça.jor.br/index.php?ed=15628>. Accessed: sep 12 2005.

_____. Available at: <http://www.omensageiro.com.br/personalidades/personalidade-2a.htm>. Accessed: jan 14 2005.

XAVIER, Francisco Cândido. *Voltei.* 21. ed. Rio de Janeiro: Federação Espírita Brasileira, 2001.

AB Editora
Cultura e Qualidade

Vendas: (62) 3219-8600
Informações: (62) 3219-8696
Fax: (62) 3219-8644

www.abeditora.com.br
abeditora@abeditora.com.br • livros@abeditora.com.br

Rua 15, n. 252 • Centro • CEP: 74030-030 • Goiânia-GO